Praise for
The Shape of Things to Come

"Rick Oliver has done a superb job! An unusually prescient piece of work."

GERALD J. BUTTERS
Group President, Optical Networking
Lucent Technologies Inc.

"In his stimulating overview of the past, present and future business environment, Dr. Oliver has provided executives with an invaluable source of ideas and guidelines for assessing how to transform their companies, product lines and market opportunities for the 21st Century."

KEN McLENNAN
President
Manufacturers Alliance for Productivity and Innovation

"A *must read* for every business manager and investor—in fact everyone who hopes to survive and succeed in the new economy."

DAN COHOLAN
Vice President, Technology and Communication Practice
and Director, Royal Bank/Dominion Securities

THE SHAPE
OF THINGS
TO COME

Other BusinessWeek Books

Mastering the Art of Creative Collaboration
Robert Hargrove

Conquering Uncertainty
Theodore Modis

TransCompetition
Harvey Robbins and Michael Finley

The Market Makers
Daniel F. Spulber

Asia Falling
Callum Henderson

THE SHAPE
OF THINGS
TO COME

SEVEN IMPERATIVES FOR WINNING IN THE NEW WORLD OF BUSINESS

RICHARD W. OLIVER

 BusinessWeek Books

McGraw-Hill
New York   San Francisco   Washington, D.C.   Auckland   Bogotá
Caracas   Lisbon   London   Madrid   Mexico City   Milan
Montreal   New Delhi   San Juan   Singapore
Sydney   Tokyo   Toronto

Library of Congress Cataloging-in-Publication Data

Oliver, Richard W.
   The shape of things to come : seven imperatives for winning in the
new world of business / Richard W. Oliver.
      p.   cm.—(Business Week books)
   Includes index.
   ISBN 0-07-048263-2
   1. International business enterprises—Management.
2. International economic relations. 3. Customer services—
Management. 4. Export marketing—Management. 5. Business
forecasting. I. Title. II. Series.
HD62.4.039 1998
658'.049—dc21   98-8119
                                         CIP

McGraw-Hill

A Division of The McGraw-Hill Companies

1 2 3 4 5 6 7 8 9 0 DOC/DOC 9 0 3 2 1 0 9 8

ISBN 0-07-048263-2

*The editing supervisor for this book was Jane Palmieri, and the
production supervisor was Clare Stanley. It was set in Fairfield
by Renee Lipton of McGraw-Hill's Professional Book Group
composition unit.*

Printed and bound by R. R. Donnelley & Sons Company.

To Susan

CONTENTS

PREFACE

My perspective on the shape of things to come is based on 30 years in business and academia, some 25 of which were spent with Du Pont and Northern Telecom (now Nortel), two world-class global organizations. I had the good fortune to be involved in the strategy, operations, and marketing of these two companies. Because of the nature of their products and position early in the supply chain, i.e., they sell primarily to other companies, who in turn sell to other companies and end-users consumers, I saw first-hand the strategies and operations of literally hundreds of companies, their customers, and their customers' customers. Many of those companies are world-class operators and global leaders in their fields.

My instincts about this new world of business have been further sharpened by service on the boards of directors or as a senior advisor to a number of companies that are successfully breaking past the constraints of the old logic of business and testing their mettle in the new. As a matter of principle, I will confess a "conflict of interest," since the accomplishments of several of them—Applied Innovation, Corporate Supply Network, First Union National Bank of Tennessee, Investment Scorecard, SLC Corp., and SymmetriCom—found their way into this book, although anonymously. My real-world experience has been tempered and shaped by exposure to some of the best minds in the academic world. During the 1980s and early 1990s, I was an adjunct professor at the Owen Graduate School of Management at Vanderbilt University. In addition to teaching and research, I participated in a multidisciplinary team of leading faculty specialists (international economics, strategy, finance, marketing, and operations) and students involved in the research and analysis of competitor nations and their companies. While our "stateside" secondary research was extremely valuable, the greatest insight resulted from on-site trips to four continents and dozens of countries and literally hundreds of interviews with leading executives and government officials.

In addition to serving as a member of the faculty at the Owen School, where I teach corporate strategy and global business, in the early nineties I formed Global Market Associates to assist companies in managing the transition to the new world of business. My goal in these activities is to provide students and business organizations with a perspective on the relentless pace of change created by globalization and technology. Thus, my views have been conditioned by business experience, by discussions with practitioners in many corporate functions, and by discourse with leading academicians at the Owen Graduate School of Management and elsewhere.

Together with my own experiences, research, and observations, this material has been processed into seven strategic imperatives for coping with the new world of business.

Part 1, The Shape of Things Past, provides the reader with a historical view of changes during the past several hundred years that resulted in our recent arrival at the outskirts of the "global village." It begins with the explosive changes created by new technologies and globalization and sets the stage for the new empowerment that individuals, organizations, and even countries inherited as citizens of the global village.

Part 2, The Shape of Things Today, describes the contours of the new business space developing from the "implosion" created as these technologies and globalization reach their peak. Just as sound only becomes "visible" on the wings of a jet as it is about to break the sound barrier, so too are the effects of these forces visible just as they reach their maximum velocity and impact. Thus Part 2 describes the now extant "twenty-first century customers," and their short but compelling list of demands (speed, quality, variety, service, and price). Part 2 also argues that this twenty-first century customer has created a new set of market dynamics that require major changes in the way companies go to market. Despite its title, Marketing in the Global Village, the final chapter of Part 2 argues that there are no longer any markets in the traditional sense, only customers. It describes the key characteristics of the global village market*space*.

We have shifted dramatically away from the Industrial Age paradigm of "cogs in the wheel," in which we were at the mercy of industry, so to speak, to the immensely more powerful position of being "nodes in the network," able to influence as well as be influenced by events. How individuals and organizations can win in this new world of business is suggested in Part 3, The Shape of Things to Come. Chapter 7 discusses the seven key imperatives for winning in this new economic space. To support the argument, I also cite seven organizations I call "twenty-first century companies" (including the U.S. military) that appear to embody the ingredients necessary to succeed into the next millennium. To that list I add my pick of seven products, "twenty-first century products," that will help sculpt the new shape of things to come. Chapter 8 is a brief discussion of the new shape of retail and the need to rethink every aspect of business. In Chapter 9, I speculate about the economic engine for the near-term future—biotechnology and new materials—that will create a "post-information society," a period that I believe will be characterized by unprecedented stability, wealth, and growth. Finally, in the Epilogue, I forecast what I think the economic eras beyond biotechnology and new materials will look like, circa 2050.

In keeping with my views about the dynamics of the global village, readers should be able to move through this book fairly quickly. I have labored to be as succinct as possible, to present ideas in a fashion that can be understood with illustration rather than "proof" in an academic sense. My purpose in writing the book is to bring coherence and context to the major forces reshaping our lives. I offer the results as one person's educated guess about the future.

Richard W. Oliver

OWEN GRADUATE SCHOOL OF MANAGEMENT
VANDERBILT UNIVERSITY
NASHVILLE, TENNESSEE

ACKNOWLEDGMENTS

This book is about the future, the shape of things to come. No person has the ability to predict the future with any certainty, but we know from past experience that teams of people—people with knowledge, imagination, sensitivity, and wisdom—working closely together can provide deep insight into the likely course of events. I've been blessed to be part of such a team. Although this book carries my name, it really belongs to the team: in Nashville—DeeGee Lester, Kim Brothers, Norman Moore, Susan Oliver, William Taylor, Danny Sulkin, Antonina Marinova, Eimear O'Connell, Kim Ward, and Beryl Brothers; at PMA—Peter Miller and Yuri Skujins; and at McGraw-Hill—Mary Glenn and Kurt Nelson. Special recognition is due Edmund Fitzgerald, former Chairman and CEO of Northern Telecom, from whom I learned so much about the global marketplace; Marty Geisel, Dean of the Owen School, who supported this effort in numerous ways; Roland Rust, my colleague at Owen, with whom I collaborated to develop the ideas on the future of advertising and adaptive products; and Shawn Cartwright, a student at Owen with whom I worked on the concept of value webs. I also acknowledge here my deep gratitude to Marshall McLuhan, a teacher who taught me to see things in exciting new ways. All have functioned variously as teachers, researchers, editors, thinkers, and most important, insightful challengers of conventional wisdom. Thank you.

Credit goes as well to the literally thousands of people in companies around the world to whom I listened and talked. Together, we brought into focus the shape of things to come.

A final thanks goes to McGraw-Hill whose Business Week Books idea makes this volume possible.

THE NEW WORLD OF BUSINESS

Rapid globalization and technological change have affected the lives of every person involved in business for at least the last half of this century. Very simply, this book is about the aftermath, the chaos, left in the wake of the enormous confluence of globalization and technology, particularly, information technology. Neither force alone, globalization nor technology, could have created this new world of business, but together they have revolutionized the environment for every individual, business, and organization around the world. I refer to this new world of business as a "global village." In addition to portraying the chaos inherent in the global village, I'll describe means by which individuals and organizations can survive and succeed.

This is not a book about the wonderful things created by the Information Age. In fact, as I assert in Chapter 2, we are essentially at the end of the Information Age.

This does not imply that information or information companies that supply telecommunications, software, computers, the Internet, and the like are no longer important. They remain as important today as Industrial Age companies that produce steel, cars, and airplanes. Like energy, information will continue to be essential to our economic lives. But information will not be the engine that drives and shapes the future economy. Information companies, particularly hardware producers, are near the mature phase of their life cycle, and the shape of their world is clear: Rivalry is intensifying; they compete increasingly on price; and technological development is in applications rather than in new science.

Hardware electronics companies were the fastest growing and ultimately the largest employers of the late 1970s and 1980s, but they have been downsizing dramatically. The new growth is in information applications (e.g., software and electronic services), just as the growth in services supporting Industrial Age products grew dramatically at the end of that era. For business, the energy of the Industrial Age, coupled with the global electronic embrace of the information hardware and software of the Information Age, has had the effect of abolishing the constraints of both time and space.

The new economic engine that will soon power the new world of business is bio-materials (see Chapter 8, Every Cell a Factory). Our entry into the Age of Bio-Materials—biotechnology and the exciting world of new materials—holds the promise of gaining control over matter. In many ways then, this book is about how the Industrial Age made us one world, the Information Age made us one village, and how bio-materials will make us one family. Obviously, such transformations have enormous implications for business.

One of the key ideas embedded in the notion of the global village is that everything seems to happen at once and in a very intimate way, no matter where in the world it occurs. Granted, it would be easier to deal with issues and events at arm's length, independently and sequentially, but in the global village things just don't happen one by one, in turn, or in isolation. They happen simultaneously, interdependently, and in force, in a word, *chaotically*. This chaos is a natural result of the electronic speed of the new world of business mingling with the flotsam of industrial markets. It is analogous to the disruption and disorientation surely felt by those who lived the transition from agrarian to industrial economies, and what we in the industrialized world felt during the difficult transition from an industrial to an information-based economy. This is the new world of business, and its early forms at least are not hard to discern. However, its shape and evolution will not come easily for those accustomed to the more structured world of industrial markets.

Business in the global village is complex and moves very quickly, and many issues must be dealt with holistically and in an integrated fashion. Obviously, it would be easier to dissect and address business problems and concerns into more manageable pieces. There are many books that help do so, but this book presents the broad sweep of economic, political, and cultural affairs, the interrelationships between those realms, and a holistic approach to dealing with them. The goal is to provide organizations and individuals with a greater understanding of how the global village was created, the interrelationship of the attendant issues, and usable strategies for success.

Much of what is taking place doesn't resonate well with those schooled in the old world of business. For my part, I make no value judgments. I simply try to establish the contours of this new world and detail the guiding forces that create its form. As such, this book is devoted as much to the "edges" that create the shape of this new world as to the great mass of its center.

THE SHAPE OF THINGS PAST

The Shape of Things Past begins with the events of Tienanmen Square in mid-1989, and then recounts the massive changes of the last half of the twentieth century as globalization and technology combined to create a "global village." What ended with the Tienanmen story began with Neil Armstrong's historic landing on the moon, July 20, 1969, because Armstrong's lunar landing was the last great achievement of the Industrial Age, while Tienanmen announced the maturity and growing power of Information Age technologies.

Although the telephone and telegraph date from the second half of the 1800s, the Information Age actually began on December 23, 1947, with the development of the transistor at Bell Labs in Basking Ridge, New Jersey. Subsequent innovations would lead to solid-state microelectronics and today's ubiquitous computer chip, which is now being produced globally at the rate of nearly a billion per minute and is found in everything from supercomputers to inexpensive children's toys.

The Shape of Things Past describes how the explosive changes of the Industrial Age combined with the implosive changes of the Information Age to remake the geopolitical world. Governments became economically powerless, ethnicity replaced nationalism as political motivation, and traditional economics were rendered irrelevant.

For business it was the period when markets became global, skyscrapers crumbled, corporate hierarchies flattened, the role of the CEO was redefined, and logistics replaced quality and price as a key corporate battlefield. In effect, the world turned upside down.

THE WORLD
TURNED
UPSIDE DOWN

During May and early June of 1989, the world was stunned by daily images of Chinese students crowding into Beijing's Tienanmen Square demanding democratic reforms. Modern interactive telecommunications technology, e.g., satellites, faxes, and advanced long-distance telephone services such as direct dialing, made possible what *Newsweek* called a "revolution by information." Although government forces crushed the Chinese student revolt, the message to all governments, not just the Chinese, was clear: Interactive communications technology empowers human activity by providing direct access to others and to information and events anywhere in the world. Although early Information Age technologies like radio and TV were important in laying the groundwork for change, it was the interactive technologies that made such empowerment possible. It was the clearest announcement to date, in case anyone missed the earlier ones, that the world had turned upside down.

Within the next few months, the world witnessed the destruction of the Berlin Wall, the fall of communism throughout Eastern Europe in the autumn of 1989, and the dismantling of the Soviet Union by 1991. The long-dreaded direct conflict between the United States and the Soviet Union's "evil empire" never materialized. Instead, during the early postwar period, the U.S. military fought "proxy wars" in Korea and Vietnam. As the

Cold War period drew to a close, American soldiers saw action in places like Granada, Panama, Haiti, and Iraq. The overriding power of electronic technologies changed the location and even the shape of U.S. "enemies." Moreover, it changed both the international and internal balance of power for the superpowers and the futures of every other country, large and small.

Since the end of the Cold War, old enemies such as the Israelis and the PLO and the North and South Koreans have moved to the negotiating table, while former political prisoners Vaclav Havel (Czech Republic) and Nelson Mandela (South Africa) rose to the presidencies of their countries. And in stark contrast to the power enjoyed by the major trading nations in the chummy country club structure of the Organization for Economic Cooperation and Development (OECD), or the unenforceable rule-making of the General Agreement on Trade and Tariffs (GATT), even the smallest country carries the same vote as the largest in the world's new trade democracy, the World Trade Organization (WTO). Unlike GATT, WTO rules are enforceable.

New information technologies constantly outstripped governments' ability to regulate or control them. As a consequence, most governments around the world moved dramatically away from the regulation of markets, particularly technology-oriented ones, with deregulatory actions and market liberalizations the impact of which was ultimately as far-reaching as the fall of communist and right-wing regimes. The United States has already deregulated transportation, telecommunications, and electrical power, among others things; the European Union (EU) eliminated the restrictions on using domestic suppliers to carry telecom traffic, attempting to create the world's most liberal telecommunications market; and Latin American governments are deregulating everything that moves. The WTO is working to take these deregulatory initiatives worldwide.

New electronic technologies likewise altered forever a constant of domestic governmental power: influence over, if not effective control of, information. The political upheaval of the late 1980s and early 1990s demonstrated government's inability to control advances in interactive telecommunications that tie people together. Political leaders, even in nations as powerful as the United States, realized that power also exists at unofficial levels. Power now knew no borders; it belonged to everyone. Powerful new voter coalitions and dissidents and activists of all kinds easily bypassed "official channels" to relay information and influence events a world away. But it's not just dissidents usurping government control of information. Organized religious groups now use the Internet to spread their messages, sometimes in defiance of governments, just as underground printers in the old Soviet Union produced and distributed bootleg Bibles.

Nowhere was the loss of power of the nation-state more apparent than in international financial markets. As Walter Wriston, former Chairman of Citicorp, said in a 1998 interview in *Wired* magazine about why the power of the state is in decline.

WIRED: Is stateless money moving around the world with increased velocity?

WRISTON: No question about it. What annoys governments about stateless money is that it functions as a plebiscite on your policy. There are 300,000 screens out there, lit up with all the news traders need to make value judgments on how well you're running your economy. Before the Euromarket and floating exchange rates, the president could go into the Rose Garden and make a statement about the dollar, and the world would quietly listen. Today, if the president goes into the Rose Garden and says something dumb, the cross rate of the dollar will change within 60 seconds. This creates what I call the information standard. The information standard is more draconian than the gold standard, because the government has lost control of the marketplace. It overwhelms it.

WIRED: As the power of sovereign governments wanes, who is left in charge?

WRISTON: Everybody.

The democratizing and decentralizing power of interactive information technologies created similar power shifts between and within corporations. When their traditional hierarchical pyramids flattened, corporate information and control dispersed among myriad stakeholders, from customers and suppliers to investors, employees, and corporate activists. No sooner had management flattened the corporation than outside "experts" began calling for radically new organizational models, such as "the donut" (first described by Charles Handy in *The Age of Paradox*). With a core of key people, an outer ring of suppliers, specialists, consultants, temps and part-time employees, and outsourced jobs, the thinking behind the donut is to be able to move people in and out of the organization as needed.

But new organizational structures are not the only manifestations of industrial power turned upside down by new technologies. Even the skyscraper, long the architectural symbol of corporate hierarchy, began to fall under the "information wrecking ball." The industrial revolution not only gave us power over the outer space of Neil Armstrong but also the inner space of corporate architecture. The sample—by today's standards at least—technology of the elevator created the ability to give physical expression to the notion of centralized corporate hierarchy. But the Industrial Age's *vertical* model gave way to the *horizontal* corporate campus as organizations flattened and hierarchies and buildings tumbled.

The Industrial Age was a period of increasing centralization of nations, cities, and companies. It created both the need for and the ability to construct hierarchical organizations and centralized management housed in huge skyscrapers. The Information Age created the necessity and the means to do the opposite, flatten organizations and spread them out across acres of two-story villagelike huts linked together by e-mail. In fact, just as the elevator created the power to build centralized management hierarchies into the sky, e-mail has created the wherewithal to stretch management across the planet. While an Industrial Age company like General Motors tries doggedly to battle against vast market changes from its lofty office tower in Detroit, an Information Age company like Microsoft wires into fast-changing global market events from a huge campus of networked low-rises in a Seattle suburb. Industrial Age technologies pushed organizations *up at the centers*; Information Age technologies pushed them *out to the margins*.

Regardless of the shape of the organization or its physical manifestations, corporate power decentralized. Many organizations adopted the "tangerine strategy" of breaking into component parts. Others, usually large ones, attempted to combat the fast-changing scale and scope of the global and technological marketplace by getting even larger. And still others tried to do both at once, organizing into smaller, stronger units within a "confederation," to provide the benefits of scope and scale. The result was that even the smallest market participant had increased power.

Some CEOs, however, clung to pre-World War II paradigms of hierarchical leadership and delayed responding to the rapidly changing demands of their constituents. Many of these corporations found themselves confronted on all sides by increased competition and powerful, vocal stakeholders. In the United States, former CEO of Metropolitan Fiber Systems James Crowe put it best: "The day of the imperial CEO is gone." CEOs in every industry surely recognize the truth of that prediction after witnessing the long list of unceremonious public departures of corporate leaders: John Akers (IBM), Robert Stempel (GM), James Ketelson (Tenneco), Tom Barrett (Goodyear), Kenneth Olsen (Digital Equipment), Rod Canion (Compaq Computer), Paul Lego (Westinghouse), and Bob Allen (AT&T).

If the sinecure CEO's position has become tenuous, the market security of corporate superpowers has been stomped. Some of the corporate Goliaths of the 1970s—IBM, General Motors, Sears—found themselves by the 1980s spiraling in downturns and besieged on all sides by upstart Davids. Morgan Stanley's rankings in 1972 listed IBM (#1), General Motors (#2), and Sears Roebuck (#6) among the world's leaders in stock market valuation. Twenty years later, the three companies ranked 26th (IBM), 40th (GM), and 81st (Sears) and were frequently derided as dinosaurs in dramatic decline. By 1997, *Business Week's* annual Global 1000 showed some recovery for IBM (13th, up from 20th the year before), but GM was 53rd (down from 36th in 1996) and Sears had fallen to 174th. On the other hand, Microsoft, founded in 1975 and incorporated in 1981, was ranked number five in the world, behind only global giants and perennial superstars GE, Coca-Cola, Royal Dutch-Shell, and the Japanese telecommunications company NTT. Other giants— Xerox, 3M, Ford, and Eastman Kodak among them—had similar experiences and saw the need for change, although apparently not fast enough for Kodak, as it continued to struggle with nimble Fuji.

Many other companies, however, have found ways to transform their lumbering bureaucracies into big company-small company hybrids, combining the financial clout and research and distribution capabilities of a large organization with the flexibility, speed, and customer focus of the entrepreneur. The world turned upside down demonstrated that three common characteristics would guide the leading corporations of the future: (1) an emphasis on decentralized management with a small central staff, (2) minimal vertical integration, and (3) a heightened focus on core products and customers. Some, like IBM, have used this formula to forge dramatic turnarounds. It's akin to how General Charles Krulak, commander of the U.S. Marine Corps, describes the Corp's new strategy of vesting the fighting force in the field with increased power and decreasing centralized command: "A whole lot of teeth, and very little tail."

The challenge to corporate power extended beyond size to questions of strategic flexibility with the advent of a whole new genre of public concerns. Around the United States, for example, public opinion challenged the building of Wal-Marts, and even powerful Disney encountered public ire following the announcement of plans to build a theme park near the Antietam battlefield site in Virginia. In other areas, health-conscious Baby Boomers forced fast-food chains to provide nutritional information and revise their menus to reduce the fat content. Likewise, the Phen-fen scare among dieters resulted in greater consumer concerns about health products and diet supplements, leading eventually to a Phen-fen ban. Powerful tobacco companies, such as RJR and Philip Morris, struggled for survival against declining consumer numbers, mounting lawsuits, revelations regarding industry knowledge of health risks, increased efforts to regulate consumption through antismoking legislation, and proposed tax increases on cigarettes to fund health care.

The world also turned upside down for giant steel companies and automakers, traditionally among the most powerful industries. Beginning in the 1970s, technology and globalization turned the steel industries of the industrial West on their heads. Once powerful steel companies in the United States, European Union, and even Japan experienced serious dislocations related to growth, trade flows, and foreign investment. Steel is historically a domestic product, but since WWII, steady globalization and technological change has pushed international product flows to the point that some one-fourth of all steel production now crosses an international border. Much production has shifted to the developing parts of Eastern Europe, Asia, and South America. According to a recent OECD report, "Whatever [steel production] growth occurs in industrialized countries will probably not come from large integrated producers, but from smaller, more efficient minimills." For the United States, global competition transformed a dynamic steel region into a "rust belt."

In the auto manufacturing sector the old adage, "What's good for General Motors is good for the USA," had become laughable. GM was losing money on almost every car and truck sold in the United States. Ford and Chrysler car sales were in decline as well. In 1955, U.S. automakers had a 100 percent share of the U.S. car market. Now, their share has dropped to below 60 percent. The U.S. Department of Commerce's *U.S. Global Trade Outlook 1995–2000* placed foreign imports at 32 percent. That, combined with their U.S.-based production, gives foreign-owned automakers more than 40 percent of the U.S. market.

Most recently, the reality of a world turned upside down demonstrated itself in global financial markets as the celebrated "Asian Miracle" turned into "Asian Flu." The Asian engine for global economic growth appeared headed for total collapse in late 1997 amid regional stock market plunges, currency devaluations, and the failure of financial institutions, including one of Japan's "Big Four," Yamaichi Securities. The crisis prompted bailout efforts by global organizations such as the International Monetary Fund (IMF) and the 18-member Asian-Pacific Economic Cooperation Organization to prevent further impact on world markets. This crisis in Asia, although of great importance at the moment, should prove to be simply a temporary phenomenon. It does demonstrate, however, how interdependent the world's economies have become and the value of global institutions guiding transitions into the future.

Throughout history, the world has experienced many revolutions in culture, economics, politics, and social norms. None of them, however, seem as dramatic and all-encompassing as those of the last half-century. The world has truly turned upside down. Few, if any, of the social, political, cultural, and economic "truths" with which we exited WWII remain valid as we enter the twenty-first century. No country, no Fortune 500 company, no individual has escaped the extraordinary impact of technology and globalization of the past 50 years.

GLOBALIZATION AND TECHNOLOGY

In his plainspoken way, Harry Truman used to say that the only thing about the future that you couldn't predict was the history you didn't know. So while this book is essentially about the future, it is prudent to take Truman's advice and look to history as a guide to where we'll be tomorrow.

ECONOMIC LIFE CYCLES

Exhibit 2.1 charts the life cycles (in the form of "S curves" similar to those of product life cycles) of the three major economic eras—agrarian, industrial, and information—over the past 3000 years. It graphically illustrates a major contention of this book: that the early 1990s marked both the pinnacle and the maturity of the Information Age. Lasting little more than 56 years, the Information Age entered its mature phase in the late 1980s and, for all practical purposes, ended with Marc Andreessen's development in 1993 of Mosaic, the first user-friendly adaptation of Tim Berens-Lee's World Wide Web.

Before probing more deeply into the globalization and technologies of the Information Age, several quick points will help underline the main ideas of Exhibit 2.1.

Economic eras follow an "S" curve life cycle.   The life cycles of an economy exhibit many of the same characteristics associated with the four stages of a product life cycle: inception,

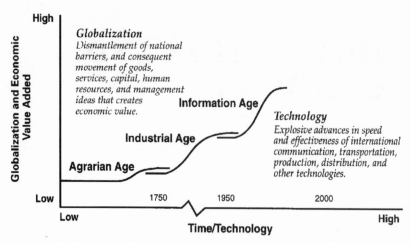

EXHIBIT 2.1.   Two major forces create the global village: technology and globalization. (*CSC Index. Reprinted by permission. All rights reserved.*)

growth, maturity, and decline. However, the maturity and decline of an economic era do not imply its disappearance, since we still need the output of agriculture, and Industrial Age products such as automobiles are still a vital part of our economy. But it does mean that the *engine* of economic value added, growth, and employment has changed.

Today, for example, more people are employed in Information Age businesses than in Industrial Age businesses. However, Information Age businesses are increasingly under cost and productivity pressure, and the electronics industry, once the largest employer in the United States, is shrinking rapidly in terms of overall employment.

The changing nature of the economy is reflected in U.S. employment figures. At the end of the nineteenth century, 93.5 percent of Americans were employed in agriculture and fishing; 5.7 percent in manufacturing, construction, and mining; and less than 1 percent in services. At the end of the twentieth century, those numbers are nearly reversed, with 73 percent employed in service industries, nearly 25 percent in manufacturing, and only 2.9 percent in agriculture. This is even more dramatic, considering the fact that the majority of those employed in manufacturing are really service workers (sales, service, R&D, engineering, etc.) and not direct factory workers. Other western nations have followed similar patterns. Rather than eliminating jobs, new technologies tend ultimately to create increasing amounts of better-paying, more knowledge-intensive work, albeit in different commercial areas. As we exit this century, the United States should have about the same number of people employed in service industries as it had in both agriculture and manufacturing when it entered the century. The percentages employed in agriculture and manufacturing at the end of the twentieth century will about equal those employed in service and knowledge industries at the start of the twenty-first century.

Clearly, there are those who are left behind in such transitions. In earlier times, during the transition from the Agricultural Age to the Industrial Age, workers made an easier adjustment, because the prime commodity was physical rather than mental strength. In the conversion to an information economy, the dislocation for workers was more acute because the major change was from physical to mental work. Those without an education suffered most.

Economic cycles are getting steeper and shorter. The Agrarian Age covered many centuries, but the Industrial Age lasted only about 200 years, and the Information Age lasted little more than 50 years. This trend helps to bear out, at least in part, the increasing rate of change in the last half of the twentieth century. In fact, living Americans born before 1950 are the first generation in history to live through both the beginning and the end of an economic era!

The technology of each new economic era transforms everything that came before it. The mechanical "muscle" power of Industrial Age technologies revolutionized agriculture, and the intellectual brainpower of Information Age technologies (robotics, CAD/CAM, etc.) is now revolutionizing manufacturing around the world. Thus, we can expect the technologies of the future similarly to transform information, industrial, and agricultural technologies.

Economic eras create conventional wisdom that is often hard to reconcile with the dynamics of a new era. This is particularly true during the time of initial transition. Early in the Information Age, it was difficult to shake the conventional wisdom of the Industrial Age. New ideas seemed like "logical inconsistencies." For example, the Information Age manufacturing paradigm of mass customization was virtually impossible to reconcile for those unable to see beyond the Industrial Age paradigm of mass production. And while many cling to the Industrial Age idea of economies of scale, its importance has been eclipsed by the importance of economies of scope. In the Information Age, it is not the scale of an enterprise that counts, but its scope—the ability to craft products or services for specific customers.

A mature industry or economy is marked by a number of factors:

1. A significant number of companies offering technologically similar products intensely competing for a large market
2. Pervasive price competition
3. Extensive diffusion of products
4. Focus on product applications and process improvements rather than on "new science"

The metrics of the aging of the Information Age are clearly evident: computers, most with modems, in 45 percent of homes and almost every office in the United States; on-line and Internet connectivity to nearly 40 million Americans and almost as many worldwide; several thousand companies competing for a trillion dollar market, in some cases with barely distinguishable products; some 10 thousand chips for a dollar (compared to a dollar a piece in 1960); almost-free cell phones and sophisticated computers for under $800. The computer chip has become the most ubiquitous product in history. No one, however, is seriously discussing a replacement for the chip, and the semiconductor industry is focused almost exclusively on process improvements, with an industrywide agreement on design, powering, cooling, and process improvements extending to 2010.

By the mid-1980s Information Age computer hardware companies were dealing with the problems experienced by Industrial Age companies little more than a decade earlier: too much competition, too many employees, high cost structures, etc. And as *Business Week* reported in early 1998, between 1993 and 1997, employment in the computer and chip industries rose only slightly (from 54 million to 61 million), whereas revenues quadrupled, from $56.5 billion to $208.9 billion, and productivity (in terms of thousands of dollars per employee) rose from 104.0 to 342.3 in the same period.

Such numbers demonstrate that the "value-added" of an economic era is greatest at its maturity. Productivity gains from information technology will continue unabated, just as those from Industrial Age technologies helped fuel postwar growth in the Information Age. But while the Information Age will not be the major engine of economic growth of the future, it clearly defined much of the shape of things past.

GLOBALIZATION AND TECHNOLOGY: FROM HUNTING AND GATHERING TO THE INFORMATION AGE

The economic activities of the earth's first people were largely confined to hunting and gathering food. Each person or small group hunted and gathered enough just to sustain life. There was little specialized work and little or no trading. Obviously, these rudimentary activities created little *economic value added*, that is, economic value beyond that needed to sustain an individual life. "Technology" was largely limited to crude instruments for killing game.

The next economic era, the Agrarian Age, began when crude hunting instruments were applied to the cultivation of crops. This technology change created a new economy based on agriculture, although even late in this era, farmers continued to perform tasks by hand in much the same way as their forebears. They were aided to some extent by a limited number of crude, animal-powered implements, but there was very little economic value added, since farmers grew little more than what their own families consumed. Nonetheless, the first trading and specialization (globalization) began to appear as early Egyptians gathered on the Nile to exchange goods with the Phoenicians. This trade created only a small increase in economic value added, but it improved the lot of many people. Near the end of the Agrarian Age, improved farming methods (crop rotation and increased use of fertilizers) contributed to a dramatic increase in agricultural production. However, the average farmer could still plant and harvest only about 10 to 12 acres per year.

The invention of the new technologies that ushered in the Industrial Age—about 1750, first in England, then Germany, and finally in the United States—transformed agriculture and expanded per-acre yield, replacing processes and animal-powered implements with increasingly sophisticated, self-powered machinery. Between 1840 and 1890, the required time to harvest one bushel of wheat tumbled from 3 hours to 10 minutes.

Despite the doubling of U.S. land under cultivation and a dramatic rise in population (from 31,400,000 in 1860 to 63,000,000 in 1890), improvements in agricultural technology, combined with improved delivery through an expanded railway system, reduced the number of workers required to feed the nation. Agriculture achieved full mechanization by the twentieth century following the introduction of the gasoline engine and the invention of the tractor. Notwithstanding the famines that still haunt parts of the underdeveloped world (which could be cured economically, if not politically), in the Agrarian Age, *humans conquered hunger.*

Meanwhile, factory employment and production were showing dramatic increases. In production methods Ford Motor Co. had, by the early twentieth century, perfected the assembly line and reduced chassis production from 12 hours to 3. Similar advances were being made in production know-how in the United Kingdom and Germany's Ruhr Valley. Later, innovations necessary to fuel the war machines on both sides during the two world wars created advances in technological and scientific fields that were later transferred to producing both industrial and consumer products.

The economic benefits of the Industrial Age are still with us today. But the last great invention of that era, the jet engine, which ultimately created the U.S. space program and culminated with the 1969 moon landing, marked its end. Not surprisingly, the technologies of the Industrial Age created huge increases in economic value added in many national economies, and those technologies ignited the trend toward the globalization of world markets.

Writing about the Industrial Age in the past tense does not imply that there is no further innovation in this area. As with agriculture, great strides are still being made with new approaches to energy in areas such as superconductivity and cold fusion. In thermodynamics, there is even a proposition (as yet unproved and very hotly debated), that there exists a "zero-point" energy, residual energy in empty space that is ripe for harvesting. While the potential of zero-point energy can be debated, the fact remains that in the Industrial Age *humankind harnessed energy* and in so doing, *conquered space*.

THE INFORMATION AGE

A new economic era was created with the discovery of the transistor (forerunner to the microprocessor or silicon chip) in the New Jersey-based Bell Labs of AT&T in the late 1940s. Unlike the Industrial Age, which was largely a phenomenon for a very few Western nations, the Information Age was the first economic era to develop simultaneously around much of the globe. It created new wealth and economic value of unimagined proportions. It made possible new dimensions of global trade and investment and the integration of the world's economies.

The seeds of the Information Age were planted in the last half of the nineteenth century and the first half of the twentieth century with the invention of new communications technology (the telegraph, telephone, and radio) and the initial steps toward computer technology. The introduction of the Harvard-IBM Automatic Sequence Controlled Calculator in 1944 was followed in 1946 by the University of Pennsylvania's high speed ENIAC (Electronic Numerical Integrator and Calculator).

With the invention of the microprocessor, the information explosion continued with the introduction of satellites, supercomputers, software, and personal computers, which made possible the Internet, the last great innovation of the Information Age. Microprocessor technology transformed many Industrial Age businesses, first in design and manufacturing, and by now in virtually every other function.

GLOBALIZATION AND TECHNOLOGY IN THE AGE OF INFORMATION

Although Marshall McLuhan coined the term *the global village* in his 1964 book *Understanding Media: The Extensions of Man* (and Pierre Teilhardde Chardin had hinted at it a few years earlier), it officially arrived when Neil Armstrong landed on the moon in 1969. This marked the ultimate achievement of mankind's control over energy. More innovations in the energy field are eagerly awaited in the years to come, but Armstrong's achievement signaled the end of the Industrial Age and the full-scale arrival of the Information Age. The most telling "advertisement" for the introduction of this new age was the fact that the TV cameras began recording the event, allowing the world to watch Armstrong's first steps and hear his now-famous words.

As much of the world watched Armstrong step on another planet, the earth truly became a global village, owing to the confluence of the overwhelmingly powerful forces of globalization and technology. Information technology made the world a village; the economic and political forces of globalization created this village on a world scale.

GLOBALIZATION

The term *globalization* has almost become a cliché. Nevertheless, the globalization of finance, manufacturing, marketing, and management, and of political realities and social action dominates our times.

With globalization, *everything* changes, everything about how and sometimes even where and why we live our lives. And

to the revolutionary new technologies in every facet of life—
communication, travel, the production of goods and services,
logistics, and information management—there is the additional complication that these changes are taking place at alarming
speed.

In business, globalization is more than just the manufacturing, marketing, and distribution of goods and services throughout the world. It is a new way of thinking. It is the approach to
solving customer needs, no matter where in the world the customer resides. It is the segmentation of markets on a global
basis and the shift toward integrated networks and global standards. And it is the sourcing of capital, people, technologies,
and ideas from anywhere in the world.

But the globalization and rapid technological changes in
business have also brought changes in almost every other aspect
of life: culture, education, health care, social services, entertainment, religion, and politics. Improved communications,
thanks to the immediacy of satellite and cable television, the
Internet, and other interactive technologies, draws the world's
people closer together. The literature, arts, and sports of one
nation can now be shared worldwide. For example, the All-
Ireland Hurling Finals can be enjoyed everywhere. America's
pastime can reach new audiences through a 52-nation
International Baseball Association. People in China can take in
the Super Bowl while eating sushi or nachos and washing it
down with Coke.

The transformational power of globalization was felt first
and foremost in business in the 1970s and 1980s as it reshaped
commercial enterprise the world over. Today, no serious observer would argue that we have anything less than a globally interdependent economy. And although perhaps less evident,
globalization is no less powerful in other areas of life.

THE GLOBALIZATION OF EVERYTHING

Globalization of the social order means human rights and
women's issues are on the global agenda. It means that concerns about the physical environment are debated and dealt

with globally, not unilaterally by any one nation or region. In politics, globalization means the elections of Nelson Mandela, Benjamin Netanyahu, and Boris Yeltsin are as important to the world as they are in their respective countries. In medicine, it means that AIDS and the ebola virus are threats of concern to everyone on the planet. In education, globalization has shifted the focus from local and national standards of student and teacher performance to international ones.

Telecommunication and broadcast technologies render everything instantly and globally visible. When human rights were trampled in centuries past, people of the world were largely unaware. Later, with the widespread availability of print media, people became aware of such events but could remain distant and unmoved. However, with global communications media, we are forced to witness brutality, war, hunger, and environmental disasters. With instantly visible information, such matters immediately become the world's problems, problems from which we, as citizens of the world, can no longer escape.

Despite the many critics of both globalization and technology, it's important to keep in mind that these forces neither create nor solve many of these problems. They convey no moral imperative. They simply give instant, global exposure. And there is no stopping, turning back, or end point. Or as Andy Grove, Chairman of Intel, says, "Whatever can be done will be done. If not by incumbents, it will be done in a new industry born without regulation. Technology change and its effects are inevitable. Stopping them is not an option."

Globalization also means that even though most of the world's people never stray far from their homes, they are still profoundly affected. A growing percentage of today's consumers, for instance, can literally search the world for the best product, at the best price, in the configuration and time frame desired. The entire global market is but a keystroke away on the Internet.

All corporations, educational institutions, not-for-profit organizations, political parties, and even organizations that appear on the surface to be solely domestic must create survival strategies that recognize the forces of globalization.

For the individual, too, globalization means expanding knowledge, interests, and understanding beyond the parochial. The individual has truly entered the era of the global village when teens in Omaha participate in school research projects with teens in Osaka via the Internet, or when like-minded "netizens" from across the globe establish "electronic communities." There are some 70,000 on-line, special-interest discussion groups in existence that focus on issues large and small.

In some circles, globalization is viewed optimistically. It is seen as the growing interdependence of the world's economies and cultures for the betterment of all. It is believed that interdependence will reduce war and global tension and lead to a rising standard of living for humans everywhere.

But others fear globalization threatens national power and prestige. In the United States, for example, many citizens are reluctant to relinquish the notion that their country can still dominate world markets through political or economic force, exclusive American know-how, moral superiority, or a general "hunkering down." Proponents of this view call for a return to isolationism in national policy. Many in the U.S. public believe trade is a zero-sum game, and hence that concessions must be extracted before giving up any access to U.S. markets. Or as Harvard economist N. Gregory Mankiw argues, "The public's view is partly based on the false analogy that trade is like war— some countries must lose for others to win." But such concerns are not exclusive to the United States. Many other countries and regions, such as the EU, still support protectionist measures to restrict or slow trade flows, particularly in areas like agriculture.

Other critics have decried the forces propelling the "stateless" corporation. In his book, *Jihad vs. McWorld,* Rutgers University professor Benjamin Barber warns that the creation of "McWorld" spells the "end of citizenship," and argues that the expansion of global capitalism divides the world between extremes of narrow universal commercialism and factional tribalism.

What such opponents fail to realize, however, is that neither globalization nor technology is inherently good or bad. They harbor no moral or ethical points of view. Moreover, these forces are so pervasive that their true effects for good or ill are impossible to know and judge in totality. One thing is clearly true, however. These forces are too strong and too advanced to turn back. One of the undeniable realities of the global village is that no political border can hold back the flow of new ideas and technologies. Globalization is here to stay.

THE GLOBALIZATION OF BUSINESS

The globalization of industry since WWII has meant much more than just increased trade, although that was and continues to be a major component. It also involves an expanding pattern of cross-border activities, including international investment, R&D collaboration, production, sourcing, and marketing, as well as nonequity modes such as licensing and contracts. These activities create opportunities for companies to enter new markets, leverage technological and organizational advantages, and reduce business costs and risks. It is strategically quite different from the prewar pattern of exporting finished goods.

The bottom line of the globalization of business can be summed up as follows: Global trade (the movement of goods and services across borders) has grown sixfold since WWII; world trade (the volume of goods and services moving across political borders) is growing faster than world production (the rate at which the world produces goods); and foreign direct investment (FDI) (the investment in plant, equipment, and organizations by those from another country) is growing faster than world trade. Taken together, these three measures illustrate the extent and growth of globalization of the world's economy. Less easy to put numbers on, but none the less real, is the globalization of all markets.

THE GLOBALIZATION OF MARKETS CONQUERS GLOBAL POLITICS

The economics of globalization has spread rapidly and unpredictably into all aspects of life. It has altered national economic sovereignty, expanded regional power bases, and shifted the balance of power from producers to consumers and from domestic political leaders to international ones. The globalization of commerce has touched off globalization in virtually every field of human endeavor—the arts, education, medicine, unionization, entertainment, religion, and politics. Leaders in almost every part of the world have started acting in concert, recognizing that there is only one market, one standard, and one environment to be shared globally.

As with the "cargo cults" of old, much of the globalization of culture, politics, and social action has been preceded by the rapid globalization of commerce. Consider one of the world's most fractious areas, the Middle East. Despite historical antagonisms and modern problems, with deep political and cultural divisions, these nations have moved slowly but consistently toward regional peace in recognition of global economic imperatives. They appear ready to resume their historic role as the crossroads of trade and culture between Africa, Europe, and Asia.

Today, the Middle East (including Turkey, but excluding Iran and Iraq) is a large and growing market for the world's exports. Interregional trade is growing as well, evidenced by the trade pact concluded between Turkey, Egypt, Jordan and Israel, which effectively broke the Arab boycott.

The foundation of today's economic globalization was laid during the post–World War II years. For example, the General Agreement on Trade and Tariffs was established in 1946 as a formula for rebuilding global trade through the gradual elimination of trade barriers. In the latest round of negotiations, GATT became the World Trade Organization and confirmed its continued role as the global trade regulator. WTO operates much like the United Nations, with every country sharing an equal vote and with real policy-making authority over the world's trade. Other global organizations formed after the war, such as the UN, the International Monetary Fund, and the World Bank, have likewise contributed to world stability and increased global trade and investment.

A major signal in the rapid globalization of markets was the intense American-Japanese competition of the 1970s and

1980s. When General Douglas MacArthur laid the foundations of this competition in the late 1940s he summoned a small group of U.S. quality and efficiency experts to help jump-start the Japanese industrial machine.

During the 1980s, businesses around the world awoke to the realization that domestic success is inseparable from global competition, global suppliers, a global workforce, a global customer base, and a global vision. Rapid globalization created opportunities for every country to be globally competitive. By the beginning of the nineties, *Financial World*'s international issue reported that "markets for every product are growing faster than any single nation can hope to control."

Global trade now exceeds some $6 trillion. A close analysis reveals some useful information about global trade flows: most trade still occurs within a region, e.g., within the EU, NAFTA, etc.; and most interregional trade still occurs among a triad composed of Europe, Japan and the newly industrialized countries (NICs), and North America. But most of the future opportunities lie south of the equator, where populations are growing fastest, higher percentages of people are younger, and where the most rapid economic growth is occurring.

NORTH-SOUTH JOINS EAST-WEST

While trade today remains mostly east-west, future growth increasingly lies north-south. For example, during the three-day Summit of the Americas in December 1994, which included the United States and 33 Latin American nations, the "Miami Process" was initiated. The goal was to extend NAFTA and create a free trade zone from Alaska to the southern tip of Argentina by 2005. Dubbed the America Free Trade Agreement (AFTA) by some and the Free Trade Agreement of the Americas (FTAA) by others, this agreement would create the world's largest free trade zone. From a U.S. perspective, this means, for example, that Latin American markets quickly shot to the top of most everyone's list of key markets.

Recognizing this growth potential and eager to establish an early presence in Latin America, a number of U.S. companies are creating joint ventures and pursuing investment opportunities there. At the current growth rate, by the year 2000 South America should pass Europe as the major customer base for U.S. export products, while EU exports to Mercosur countries (Brazil, Argentina, Uruguay, Paraguay, and Chile as an affiliate) are growing at 40 percent per year.

Asia, too, despite the recent financial disruptions known euphemistically as the "Asian Flu," remains a fertile field for U.S. business. Already nearly one-third of U.S. exports are Asia-bound, and 60 percent of U.S. imports come from Asia. Growth in trade throughout Asia and the entire Pacific Rim is reflected in the creation of the AsiaPacific Economic Cooperation (APEC) and the Association of Southeast Asian Nations (ASEAN).

APEC's goal is to dismantle trade barriers throughout the region by 2020, but strides are already being made toward free trade in a number of areas. For example, in the fall of 1994, Malaysia took the bold step of reducing or dismantling duties on 2600 items. As a member of ASEAN (together with Indonesia, Thailand, Singapore, the Philippines, and Brunei), Malaysia is also participating in a plan to establish a common market by 2003. The goal is to reduce tariffs to less than 5 percent on most manufactured and agricultural goods.

Companies from the industrialized countries now look beyond their own borders to alternative suppliers and manufacturing in developing and former Eastern Bloc nations. The continued leveling of the playing field and the evolution of trading rules and increased trade flows are possible, in part, because many small nations are locating and pursuing manufacturing and marketing niches often overlooked by larger nations.

Meanwhile, developed countries with established manufacturing and service traditions increasingly compete in new knowledge technology and product fields such as biotechnology, robotics, computers, telecommunications, nanofabrication, civil aviation, and new materials sciences. In other words, they undertake endeavors that rely less on natural resources and more on the improved education and brainpower of a highly skilled workforce.

Globalization means that everyone has become intimately involved in everyone else's business and markets. It also means that every country large and small has an *equal* stake in the global economy and, in many ways, equal power. For example, the WTO is not just an extension of the clublike membership of GATT. Every signatory country gave up a measure of sovereignty over trade, creating a "one country, one vote" global organization with real policy enforcement power.

In 1997, a landmark WTO agreement united nations representing over 95 percent of the trade in banking, insurance, securities, and financial services under new international rules for economic stability, growth, and future development. That same year, WTO member nations also signed a global telecommunications agreement that removes tariffs on information technology products and hastens the integration of developing countries into the global trade and technology process.

Such efforts underscore a true transformation to a borderless world. And the development of a global economic infrastructure of financial services, telecommunications, and transportation, coupled with the increased importance of human and intellectual capital over natural resources and the democratization of power between nations and regions, has created a new global economic reality.

The shape of things past is clear: Globalization is not something that is coming, it is already here. There are new lessons for everyone to learn.

Lesson number one: *Globalization changes everything.*

Lesson number two: *Technology changes things in unpredictable directions.*

TECHNOLOGY

Technology is the second of the two major forces converging to create the global village.

Although there are literally thousands of new technologies and almost as many ways of categorizing them, three major technology fields, taken together, helped create the global village. The first is *information management technologies*. These include the obvious technologies of computers, software, databases, and telecommunications, and also all digital electronic information technologies, such as CD-ROM, video, sound and image technologies, digital videodisks (DVD), the rapidly growing on-line services like AOL, and network technologies (e.g., Internet).

The second I will refer to as *intelligent creation technologies*, those used in the creation and production of hard goods and service products. These technologies include such things as robotics and focused, flexible factories, mass customization, virtual reality and parallel processing, and "desktop manufacturing."

The last technological area of critical importance is *logistics* (including transportation), that is, methods for the physical movement and distribution of products and services.

As each field is examined, keep in mind that its real importance rests in the capabilities the technologies create for producers, and perhaps moreso in the expectations they create in consumers of all kinds, from goods and services—entertainment, politics, and culture.

INFORMATION MANAGEMENT TECHNOLOGY

The microprocessor, software, and digitization of information technologies are the key elements underlying all other products, technologies, and services in information management. Today, virtually all information content is either created digitally or being converted to digital form.

Enhancements in software and digital technologies roll out at an ever-faster pace. But the most dramatic improvements in cost and functionality are occurring with the microprocessor (computer chip). Originally, computer chips were glacially slow with low functionality; they now deliver almost unbelievable functionality at lightning speed. For example, in early 1998, IBM announced a new product that would double the speed and power of existing supercomputers, some 10 trillion transactions per second.

In fact, according to Moore's Law (Intel founder Gordon Moore), every 18 months, microprocessors double in power. They also experience a concomitant reduction in cost. Over the last decade, that means microprocessors experienced a one-hundredfold decrease in cost and at the same time a one-hundredfold increase in functionality.

To better understand Moore's Law, consider an example from personal computers. One of the first truly commercial PCs was the TRS-80 from Radio Shack about 15 years ago. It didn't do much, cost quite a bit ($599 for a 64-bit processor), was a true heavyweight, and was not in any sense elegant in design. By comparison, currently, a sleek portable computer, 1.2 inches thick, 4.1 pounds, 133 megahertz, active matrix color screen, 24 megabytes of RAM, and 2.1 gigabytes of memory sells for about $1300. And it fits easily onto a lap or into a briefcase.

The same dynamics of rapidly falling prices combined with equal increases in functionality and performance can be found in a telecommunication system or any other product composed largely of microprocessors. They're getting faster, smarter, cheaper, and more elegant at a dizzying speed, the result of rapid miniaturization, cost reductions from 20 to 30 percent annually in areas such as software and microelectronics, and the doubling of computer memory, processing power, and fiber optic transmission capacity every year.

These almost unfathomable dynamics underlie much of the electronic information management business. During its heyday, the 1970s and 1980s, the electronics industry was the largest employer in the United States. Because of the cost-functionality dynamics of microprocessors, however, prices dropped precipitously, putting significant pressure on margins and costs. That is why large numbers of workers began in the mid-1980s to exit electronics businesses such as AT&T and IBM. Around 200,000 employees have left IBM alone since 1988, and the departures continue today.

Despite the exodus of workers, information management technologies continue to find their way into all facets of life, from "intelligent toasters" to "intelligent roads" and "intelligent

cars." By the mid-1990s, a typical automobile had more computing power than Neil Armstrong's lunar landing craft in 1969.
In fact, the computer chip is more likely to show up in products
other than computers today.

As the computer chip became ubiquitous, virtually everything became smarter and cheaper. It will give rise to a whole
new kind of empowerment as people demand and get more and
more control over every aspect of their lives. Part Two describes
this in more detail.

It's not all hardware, though. Software is fast replacing
hardware as the key information technology, creating a whole
new world of possibilities, even a whole new language (e.g.,
applets, NCs, or network computers, *fat servers, thin clients,
browsers, websites*). *Business Week* puts the world software output at $228.2 billion, produced by more than one and a half
million workers. And software, more than hardware, drove the
development of networking. As we all increasingly connected to
the net, we graduated from the need to be merely computer literate and instead learned to be net literate.

But as we focus attention on the larger world brought to us
over the Internet, we should not lose sight of the fact that, taken
together, information technologies transformed virtually all the
products and services of daily life, rendering them smarter,
faster, cheaper, and more elegant.

INTELLIGENT CREATION TECHNOLOGIES

Intelligent creation refers to radically new ways products and
services are designed, developed, and produced, from
CAD/CAM systems (Computer Aided Design/Computer Aided
Manufacturing) to flexible, intelligent manufacturing.

Few areas have felt the impact of technology more than
manufacturing, and now services companies are experiencing
the same power with new intelligent engines of creation. Blue-
collar workers in industry after industry are finding that shop-
floor employment is heading the way that farm labor went
earlier this century. Their replacements are not scabs but robots
and other new technologies backed by new white-collar jobs in

support industries. Intelligent creation technology in manufacturing opens new capabilities in the manufacturing process and marks a dramatic shift in the potential for product customization and cost reduction.

By the beginning of the twentieth century, individualized products from craftsmen had all but given way to identical products from assembly lines. Factory output from 1900 to about 1970 was based on mass production. Armies of blue-collar workers completing repetitive tasks along assembly lines turned out identical products for mass consumption. By the 1970s, however, flexible production methodologies were joining computers and robotics to revolutionize the assembly line. The result was an expanded diversity of product lines at increased speed, reduced cost, and dramatically improved quality.

The next stage in the evolution, mass customization, uses technology to provide a low-priced product tailored to individual customer needs and specifications, all accomplished with minimal human intervention.

In this new manufacturing system, which has been variously labeled *agile, customized,* or *intelligent,* computers and robots will accept orders, determine production schedules, move parts through the process, build the products, and even perform maintenance and reprogramming of other systems. The reality of automation as replacement for factory workers is reflected in the reduction of manufacturing employees by 3.2 million since 1979, while factory output to GDP percentages remained stable. Some predictions hold that direct factory employment will about equal direct farm employment (about 1.5 percent of the population) in the very near future.

On the other hand, virtually anyone with a computer has the potential to become a one-person "desktop manufacturer." Today's sophisticated software provides the capability to conceive, design, and produce schemata for products on the desktop. Historically, one of the slowest parts of getting new products on the market was creating a prototype for testing. Current prototyping processes are often as slow as the "modeling processes" developed some 3500 years ago. A new process called *rapid prototyping* (RP) combines new digital machines and new materials to reduce prototyping time to nearly zero and save millions in costs. The market for RP machines and services had already reached more than $615 million by the late 1990s. Intelligent creation technologies are being applied to service goods as well as manufactured goods. Here, too, new software is revolutionizing the production of many standardized service goods.

The shift of manufacturing from human labor to machine-intelligent creation will gain momentum as computer and robotics techniques add capabilities for multiple, simultaneous functions. Called *parallel processing*, the theory goes like this: If two brains can perform twice the number of tasks in half the time, multiple brains can increase task capacity and reduce time needs by tens or hundreds of times. Parallel processing offers advantages beyond just speed, however. The use of more than one processor provides a level of redundancy that greatly reduces the impact of a single system failure for mission critical applications.

When fully perfected, parallel processing can unite any number of processes within a single system and assign tasks in the same way that committee assignments are given out. Computer companies are pushing this technology out of the research labs and into commercial and entertainment applications. Everything from the retail spending patterns of Wal-Mart shoppers to test programs for videos-on-demand are fodder for parallel processing experiments. It is just a matter of time until such technology is available on the PC.

As a whole, intelligent creation technologies will totally transform the creation, design, and production of products and services in the twenty-first century. These technologies mean that products and services can become not only increasingly cheaper but also closely customized to the individual needs of consumers, a truly radical concept compared to the Industrial Age mindset of mass production for a mass market.

While the possibilities for artificial intelligence excite some people, others fear the advent of smart machines will render obsolete millions of jobs. While theoretically possible, that result seems unlikely in practical terms. When computers first came into widespread use, some argued they would put millions out of work. In fact, computers created many millions of jobs and whole new industries. It's different work, surely, but work nonetheless.

Even as information technology and intelligent creation technologies became universally adopted, however, logistics technologies emerged as the new battleground for business in the global village. Price and quality were increasingly eliminated as a basis of competition. Customers got greater access to pricing information worldwide (via the Internet, for example), thus decreasing the power to differentiate on that criterion. And although the potential for short-term quality advantages for a particular supplier will always exist, the near-universal adoption of global quality standards effectively eliminated quality as a basis of long-term differentiation.

Logistics, the ability to understand customer needs and actually get the product and service in front of the customer faster than a competitor, has therefore become a critical new source of competitive advantage in the global village.

LOGISTICS

Long considered the dull, routine, less glamorous part of any business, logistics, by the late 1980s, took on a strategic role. It rose rapidly to the top of the list of corporate priorities as more and more customers demanded "time-definite" deliveries of goods and services. In fact, if quality was the business battleground of the 1980s, logistics became the battleground of the 1990s, perhaps *the* key competitive weapon in the global village.

The Gulf War offers a dramatic, though nonbusiness, example. Many marveled at the technological fighting superiority of the United States and allied military. And it was impressive, neutralizing the world's fourth largest and battle-hardened military force (they had been fighting the Iranians for several years) in less than four days! The real success story of the Gulf War was the speed and accuracy with which troops, weapons, and supplies were deployed.

The initial logistical task during the Desert Shield phase of the Gulf War involved the movement of over 120,000 troops, arms, and supplies scattered throughout the United States to the Persian Gulf region (7000 miles) in four months. But the crisis in Kuwait caught U.S. military operations in the midst of a complete overhaul of their computer systems. Lt. Gen. William G. "Gus" Pagonis, the logistics "czar" throughout the operation, coordinated a myriad of crucial tasks, ranging from deployment of vehicles, arms, and supplies to the building of latrines, procuring cold water, and setting up 10,000 Bedouin tents for the protection of troops from the 130-degree heat.

Logistical performance was a crucial factor in the ability of allied forces to conduct a successful 1000-hour air attack and 100-hour ground campaign. Although weapons technology, such as "smart-bombs," received the bulk of press and public attention during Desert Storm, many leaders in business benchmarked the military's logistics capabilities and applied the lessons to their businesses.

More than merely things with features, products are increasingly viewed as *things with features bundled with services.* Logistical excellence has become one of the most prized of those services and plays an increasingly powerful role in acquiring and keeping customers. Smart companies look for unique ways to service customers quickly through improved tracking, transporting, handling, and delivery in an effort to create what have been dubbed "logistically distinct businesses." These companies target unique customer segments and design services to meet their specific time and delivery needs. One personal computer manufacturer, for example, outsourced its replacement parts service to FedEx in order to provide overnight service to consumers for orders received even late the evening before.

Improved logistical performance depends on attention to details along the entire customer value system, including closely tracking the flow of goods, services, and information. Logistical strategies are often associated with the term "channel," indicating the need for a narrow-focused, free flow of products *and* information. The term "system" likewise emphasizes the interdependency of participants along the route. In the chaotic, interdependent marketing environment of the global village, companies are discovering unique ways to link up with partners along the value chain in two directions, suppliers at one end of the chain and customers at the other.

Logistics and transportation technologies changed everyone's idea of how fast is fast. FedEx alone has virtually eliminated the "float time" for documents and cargo. And tomorrow's technologies will prove evermore compelling. Using superconductivity for marine vehicles dramatically reduces the time for huge cargo ships to go, for example, from Tokyo to Los Angeles. Hypersonic planes have the potential to fly from New York City to Tokyo in four hours or less.

Flexible logistics-oriented organizations that use such new technologies to facilitate responsive service delivery became the hallmark for success in the early 1990s. Businesses, like military strategists, have learned that a logistics failure can derail even a brilliant product strategy. In the global village, the companies that succeed are the first to anticipate and then manifest a product or service at the customer's point of requirement.

By radically changing our perception of the possible, globalization and the technologies of information management, intelligent creation, and logistics have dramatically altered what organizations and individuals alike have to do to meet the rapidly increasing expectations of customers, employees, and stakeholders in the global village.

CHAPTER
THREE

THE GLOBAL VILLAGE

The concept of the global village seems at first glance an oxymoron. *Global,* encompassing the whole world, implies a broad, macro approach to economic, social, and political interaction among diverse nationalities and cultures. *Village,* traditionally associated with a small human community, implies a limited, micro approach; a small geographic area; and like-minded, interrelated people who unite to achieve common objectives.

Technology, particularly electronic technology, has created this logical inconsistency. Technological advances in computers and telecommunications have created global awareness of and access to information. And revolutionary advances in the efficiency and speed of production and distribution have given rise to an era in which virtually everyone has, or will soon have, access to the same high-quality, low-cost goods and services.

The globalization of business has essentially equalized the standard of living of workers around most of the developed world. The globalization of media has created a global knowledge equity, particularly about a set of desired consumer goods and political realities. The global village is therefore defined by a number of new realities:

Everyone in the world is aware of what everyone else has.

Everyone in the world aspires to the same quality products and services for the same low price, on demand.

Everyone wants these products and services customized to their individual tastes and needs.

Such new realities were made possible by the instant and interactive technologies of communications. Beginning with the telegraph, the arrival of electronic technologies sounded the death-knell for many forms of the slow, one-way print technologies (e.g., books and newspapers). The Internet may well finish the job. By the mid-1990s, most major newspapers offered electronic versions of the news, but with more speed and depth and at a lower cost to the customer. And the advent on the Internet of "push" media, the delivery of information as it happens without the need to go out and find, or "pull" it, reduced both search costs and time.

Information services offer people the immediacy of seeing and hearing events as they happen, just as in a village. Electronic information services eliminate the need for communication vehicles like newspapers, which stand to lose their audiences. A growing number of newspapers are responding by offering news on-line. *USA Today* has a free electronic version on the Internet and gets some 650,000 hits per day by Internet surfers. The newest interactive and individualized technologies have largely pushed aside even the traditional electronic media. The eight U.S. broadcast networks, for example, lost 50 percent of their market share to hundreds of narrowcasting cable networks, and in a recent poll, more than 70 percent of teenagers said they'd give up TV before giving up their computers or the Internet.

Government's ability to control the flow of information to its citizens is past as well. In the global village, thanks to improved technology, expanded satellite services to worldwide customers, and the innovative efforts of corporations, members of the world community, even those in the most remote areas, receive the same information almost simultaneously. Travelers to even the most secluded corners of the world have sent back reports of primitive villages that have a single television set somewhere near the middle, often powered by portable generators, and surrounded by eager viewers.

Ted Turner launched the first effort toward a global television network in 1980 with CNN, which was followed less than a year later by the Headline News channel. Pioneering technology, such as the "flyaway" portable satellite linkup, brought instant, worldwide coverage of news events anywhere on the globe. This flyaway capability proved invaluable with its immediate, uninterrupted coverage of crucial events such as The Gulf War, or events that grabbed global public interest, such as the trial of O. J. Simpson.

The West, particularly the United States, has been the catalyst for making many originally domestic social or political issues globally important: the environment, human and worker rights, product and work safety, racial equality, women's rights, and many more. Such issues tend to incubate on the east and west coasts of the United States, then move throughout the country and then to the rest of the world. Communications technology transcends national boundaries and nullifies traditional obstacles to access like gender, age, or socioeconomic status and creates global issues and concerns. As in the village culture of old, everyone in the global village will be instantly aware of what is happening to everyone else. Everyone will "have his nose," so to speak, "in everyone else's business." In other words, in the global village, everything is global and local simultaneously.

Thus corporate, political, cultural, religious, and social thinking in the global village take on a global dimension. Some of particular importance include:

Dramatic political moves toward democracy, liberalization, privatization, and deregulation.   Much attention in recent years has been focused on the importance of the fall of communism in the former Soviet Union and Eastern Europe. Less noticed has been an equally dramatic movement by governments throughout the world to liberalize and deregulate markets and to provide increased democracy and personal freedom. Even China has moved toward a market-based economy, perhaps foreshadowing a move to greater democracy and personal freedom. Following the demise of Soviet communism and the failure of centralized economic planning efforts worldwide, the nineties witnessed a veritable stampede to privatization. From Russia and the Eastern-bloc countries to Asia and Latin America, governments are liberalizing their economics and putting state companies on the auction block.

Development of a global consumer culture. Consumers throughout the world increasingly demand the same selection of consumer goods, particularly automobiles, clothing, many food and beverage products, and consumer durables such as appliances and electronics. For business, this global consumerism has focused sharp attention on the development of global brands, which are rapidly creating enormous brand equity positions for their companies.

Significant shifts in demographics. A complete analysis of world demography is beyond the scope of this book, but from a global business perspective, a few highlights are worthy of note.

The world's population is growing very, very fast. Population is growing at a geometric rate. The world's population reached one billion by about 1880. It took only another 85 years to reach three billion, and less than 30 more to reach five billion in 1994. The population of the world is expected to increase by another three billion by the year 2020. This, of course, has implications from a marketing standpoint. See Exhibit 3.1.

The world's population is getting older and younger at the same time. The population north of the equator is getting older. South of the equator it's getting younger. Much future opportunity for global business lies south, because that's where concentrations of young consumers will likely be for the decades ahead. It is also where you'll find the world's fastest growing incomes and most of the world's unmet needs.

The world's population is on the move. The movement of peoples throughout history has been impressive. In the 300 years from 1500 to 1800, between one and two million Europeans came to the New World, along with the forced migration of eight million Africans. During the same period,

Rank	Country	Population (in millions)
1	China	1,513
2	India	1,442
3	United States	300
4	Russia	300
5	Indonesia	286
6	Nigeria	281
7	Pakistan	267
8	Brazil	246
9	Bangladesh	235
10	Mexico	150
11	Japan	127
12	Ethopia	127
13	Vietnam	117
14	Philippines	112
15	Zaire	99

EXHIBIT 3.1. The world's largest markets by 2015.

four million Chinese migrated to China's southwest frontier. In the mid-nineteenth century, European revolutions and the Irish famine resulted in mass migrations to North America. One hundred years later, displacements resulting from WWII created migrations on a world scale. Today, major migrations still occur around the world, with some 60 million people, nearly one-fifth of the population, in motion annually. Travel and tourism is now the largest business in the world. For Japan alone, some 24 million residents visit abroad annually.

For marketers in the global village, this means that consumers identified by ethnicity may be found in any part of the globe. It also means that marketing to ethnic minorities within other dominant cultures (such as Hispanics of various kinds within the United States) becomes much more important.

Rank	City, Country	Population (thousands, projected)
1	Tokyo, Japan	28,887
2	Bombay (Mumbai), India	26,218
3	Lagos, Nigeria	24,640
4	Sao Paulo, Brazil	20,320
5	Mexico City, Mexico	19,180
6	Shanghai, China	17,969
7	New York, New York, USA	17,602
8	Calcutta, India	17,305
9	Delhi, India	16,860
10	Beijing, China	15,572

EXHIBIT 3.2. The world's largest cities by 2015.

Most of the world's economically active people live in cities. Clearly, most of the world's population is urban, and this urbanizing trend will continue as we reach the year 2000. Today's five largest cities are more populous than most countries. In the global village, therefore, the focus is increasingly on cities and not countries. Cities are rapidly becoming the key economic units of global market analysis. The 10 largest cities in the world are listed in Exhibit 3.2, the biggest of which in the future will be in the developing world. Sao Paulo, Brazil, for example, is expected to exceed three times the current population of New York City, sometime after the turn of the century.

The world's population can be divided into three broad ecological and economic groups. These groups, defined by annual per capita income and lifestyle, include:

1. **The poor**—about 1.1 billion people; household income of less than $700 per year; they earn about 2 percent of the world's income.

2. **The middle class**—about 3.5 billion people; family income between $700 and $7500 per year; they claim about 33 percent of the world's income.

3. **The consumer class**—about 1.1 billion people; household income above $7500; they account for about 64 percent of the world's income.

SIGNIFICANT SHIFTS IN POLITICAL AND SOCIAL REALMS

In addition to changing demographics, political and social changes in the global village include some startling new realities:

The rise of electronic immigrants.   Electronic immigrants, or workers who telecommute daily to provide services in countries other than their own, increasingly populate companies in the global village. Typically associated with knowledge or service work, electronic immigrants provide either advanced skills that are in short supply in the "host" country, e.g., software programming, or low-wage electronic service work. For example, programmers in Ireland, Russia, Brazil, and India are hired to write software code from instructions directed to them daily from the United States over corporate networks.

A very tangible example of the use of electronic immigrants is found in the rapid expansion of "call centers," phone or Internet services for customers to get on-line product, delivery, or other information from suppliers. A valuable service to customers and an appealing "fix" for countries suffering high unemployment, these centers use language and technical skills of one or several countries to assure 24-hour service, improved sales, and increased service to customers around the globe. U.S. companies lead in establishing call centers, although the idea is catching on worldwide. Employees of the call centers may work for a specific company or handle a variety of companies. The European call center market is adding approximately 75,000 employee positions annually, and estimates are that by the year 2001, one percent of the European workforce (about 123,000 people) will be among the electronic immigrants employed by call centers. *Business Week* reports that worldwide sales of computer software to support help desk and customer interactive software will exceed $2 billion in 1998, up from zero just five years ago.

Ethnicity is replacing nationalism.   Border guards in the old USSR frequently asked those entering the country to declare both their nationality *and* their citizenship. Such a distinction seems alien, particularly to Americans, who are accustomed to thinking of nationality and citizenship as one and the same. To many people, however, there is a stark and growing difference. And to still others, the defining attribute is neither citizenship nor nationality, but ethnicity.

Nationalism was the ultimate political expression of the technologies of the Industrial Age. The overwhelming technical forces of that economic era, such as centralization and specialization, mandated the formation of nations as a logical outgrowth of industrial economics. Before the development of factories and modern communications and transportation systems, the human community was organized primarily into tribes; there was little need for centralized government and authority. Although there were some cities, preindustrial civilization was largely a rural and village culture. Countries as nation-states are a relatively recent phenomenon in civil organization. Seventeenth and early eighteenth century maps of the world showed regions large and small comprised not of nations but of ethnic groups. The decentralizing force of information technologies may in fact reverse the move toward the nation-state, so that the map of Europe in the twenty-first century may more closely resemble the ethnic configurations of the 1700s.

This logical inconsistency of the global village suggests a duality: countries move to join supranational governance, as smaller ethnic regions move to organize politically as countries. In many parts of the world there is a growing demand for a unique *cultural space.* In the global village, a huge number of ethnic groups are uniting into new political domains. Today, the global village includes over 200 countries. In the twenty-first century, there may be as many as 500 or more. Some of this reformation of countries will happen peacefully, such as in Andorra and Czechoslovakia. Sadly, however, much will not happen without the kind of bloodshed often witnessed in Africa and the Balkans. Almost every ethnic group will push hard for their own political space—a country—different than the nineteenth-century centralizing concept of a nation (often composed of many different ethnic groups).

This trend toward ethnicity at the expense of nationalism has gained the attention of political theorists and economists as well as journalists. A controversial 1993 book, *Tribes,* by journalist Joel Kotkin, insists that transnational ethnic groups are the basis for the modern global economy. Tracing five leading ethnic groupings, Kotkin shows how extended kinship bonds lay the foundations for both emotional ties and business relations. That notion of extended kinship bonds finds its expression in twentieth-century business in, for example, the Japanese *keiretsu,* or interlocking units. Other groupings also exemplify this phenomenon. The Chinese can point to the *hua qiao,* or "overseas Chinese," numbering some 50 million. And some estimates put the Irish Diaspora at more than 70 million.

Smaller tribes are also emerging to claim their piece of the global economic pie. Among these are the Palestinians, Koreans, Armenians, and Latvians. Linked by culture, family, and religion, these ethnic groups have transcended national boundaries to create new economic, political, and marketing entities.

Hand in hand with this notion of cultural ethnocentrism is the fragmentation of political and national identity. This trend goes beyond the break-up of the Soviet Union and Eastern bloc countries, although those events focused attention on fragmentation as never before. Half of the world's countries now have a population smaller than Massachusetts. In 1914, the world contained only 62 countries; there are 209 today. Sub-Saharan Africa alone grew from 23 to 48 states between 1960 and 1964. Nor are small countries necessarily poor ones. Only two of the ten countries having more than 100 million people are economically prosperous, the United States and Japan.

On the heels of narrow voter rejection of independence for Quebec, Canadian Prime Minister Jean Chretien claimed,

"Canada is here to stay." Many, though, from politicians to business leaders, predict that this will not be the last referendum, and that the next will succeed. Quebeckers join hundreds of ethnic groups around the globe clamoring for greater political and economic participation, or political separation from the traditional nation-state. Such fragmentation of nations is sure to continue.

Two simultaneous global political movements occurred coincidentally with the arrival of the global village. On the one hand, there is an outward migration of power as countries move beyond the narrow limits of national governments to greater economic control through regional and global governance (the EU, WTO, NAFTA, etc.). On the other hand, there is the concomitant inward movement exemplified by the ethnic group identity just described. These are not mutually exclusive trends. In fact, the small group initiatives for self-determination and their confidence that they can make it economically seem to improve prospects for the success of regional economic cooperative efforts.

Economic units are getting bigger, political units smaller. While countries in the global village become smaller and more ethnically unique, the economic units to which these countries belong grow larger. Already the world's largest economic jurisdiction, the European Union (EU), will grow even larger if it admits the 12 other European countries that either have applied or are expected to apply for admission. While political alignment between eastern Europe and EU countries seems to have slowed, economic integration continues apace. For example, in less than a decade, eastern Europe's trade has shifted dramatically away from an almost total reliance on their former communist partners to more than 60 percent with the EU. North and South America undoubtedly will continue the dialogue to form a huge economic and trade bloc. And the countries of the Association of South East Asian Nations (ASEAN) are talking about further integration of their economies, though at a somewhat slower pace than in the Americas and Europe.

The globalization of citizenship.   As the global village has taken shape, a growing number of people have become aware of, and then refused to buy, a shirt or rug made by children in forced camps in developing countries. Media documentation of rights violations places additional pressure on both host nations and industries. Companies such as Levi Strauss established standards for hired foreign factories, covering everything from wages and safety issues to child labor and the right to organize. The importance of such high standards was brought home to Levi when reports surfaced that one Asian contractor was using virtual slave labor. Levi fired the contractor, thoroughly investigated the practices of all its contractors, and became the first multinational to introduce guidelines and regular inspections for all manufacturing facilities. Not all companies have demonstrated a propensity to react quickly to these new standards, and only time will tell if the marketplace will reward or punish them. Nike, for example, has made some concessions to workers' rights and more competitive wages in foreign countries, but remains under media pressure to make more changes.

Although business often displays the most visible global behavior, political parties, religious organizations, and educational institutions—in fact, all organizations and all individuals—are now held to a global standard of citizenship.

The Shape of Things Past gives the world of business a radically new profile as the confluence of globalization and technology created a phenomenon called the global village. For business, the implication is perhaps best expressed in the dictum, *"Think global—act local,"* and in the equally appealing reversal of that phrase, *"Think local—act global."* Both approaches will be necessary for success in the new world of business. In fact, as I'll assert in Part Three, the new shape of things to come includes the strategic imperative to Think Global, Act Global, a new mindset in which everything is global, from strategy and tactics to product and program execution.

THE SHAPE
OF THINGS
TODAY

To best understand The Shape of Things Today, it is important to recognize that for all practical purposes, the twenty-first century is already upon us and that the principal difference between today and the world described in Part 1 is the presence of an *informationally empowered consumer.* The distinguishing characteristic of today's consumers, twenty-first century customers, is that they are now at the front end of the business process not the back end. In effect, it is what the "theory" of business has always proclaimed but seldom practiced.

It's a radical difference in today's world of business: customers are in charge. In many ways then, we've moved from a producer to a consumer economy, or as one observer has remarked, from "the dictatorship of supply to the democracy of demand." However, we label these changes, it is information that affords this supreme power.

Much of the contour of this Part 2 is dictated by the twenty-first century customer: *what* products and services they want, *how* they want them made, *when* they want them, *where* they want them, and finally, *what* price they're willing to pay.

THE TWENTY-FIRST CENTURY CUSTOMER

Perhaps the most important thing to understand about twenty-first century customers is that they are *informationally empowered*. With that power, they *demand active engagement in the market process*. Today's "plugged in" consumers know instantly what's happening around the world, what new goods and services are available anywhere, and on what terms. In the global village, everyone wants in on the act. Consumers have power and are increasingly showing their propensity to use it. Thus two dominant notions define this "twenty-first century customer": (1) they have information parity with suppliers in today's economic marketspace and (2) they demand active engagement with producers as equal players in the marketplace.

INFORMATION EMPOWERMENT

Information empowerment means that now both retail consumers and business customers have all the information they need to make the best "value" decisions about goods and services from anywhere in the world. This is particularly true in the developed countries, but consumers in the rest of the world are not far behind. The forces of globalization and technology have created highly sophisticated global consumers who no longer accept what manufacturers and service providers tell them to buy. Instead, the world's consumers have become adept shoppers demanding that producers meet their every need.

Historically, producers, or channel intermediaries, could conceal much about a product's or service's performance, price, and value-in-use characteristics. This does not mean malice of intent. It means that out of competitive necessity, and given the option, any supplier would only divulge the positive things about their products or services. In today's world of business, consumers have information never before available. Two brief examples illustrate.

Previously, when buying a new car, a consumer entered an automobile showroom at a considerable disadvantage. Pricing of new cars was complex, from the establishment of the base price to the pricing of myriad options. Bargaining was difficult because the consumer had only a vague idea about the pricing structure. Now, publications like *Consumer Reports* offer new car shoppers a detailed analysis of pricing, including dealer invoice and associated costs, along with pricing of every option with costs and standard margins. *Consumer Reports* will fax a car buyer this information in an average time of 15 minutes.

The Internet offers even more empowerment for those wishing to buy or lease cars. Internet service providers offer access to car information sources ranging from used and antique car parts suppliers and automakers' home pages to a host of information services, including *Consumer Reports*. Internet sites assist buyers with information on pricing, the range of customized options, and so on in a setting removed from the pressure of the sales floor. In addition, financial web services give potential buyers assistance calculating costs and even negotiating agreements with car dealers. Armed with such knowledge, the informed consumer gains new confidence for what used to be a very stressful ordeal.

The second example comes from one of life's most perplexing problems, legal fees. Savvy business customers, no longer content with accepting huge bills with limited documentation about hours spent on a client's legal affairs, are demanding and getting on-line access to their lawyers' in-house computers in order to track billable hours.

This kind of empowerment comes courtesy of a global communications infrastructure that assures anyone access to any kind of information about a product or service anywhere in the world. The growing information empowerment of consumers was vividly brought home several years ago from the world of geopolitics. As most of the world was glued to the television watching the mounting tensions between the United States and Iraq on CNN, people around the world discovered at the very same instant as Saddam Hussein that the Gulf War had started. He too found out while watching CNN. For the first time in history, everyone in the world watched the start of a war, including one of the principal combatants.

Though less dramatic than the Gulf War, that kind of empowerment in the commercial context means that any customer anywhere in the world, at any time, has the potential to know as much as the supplier—about goods and services, pricing, product availability, financing options, and competitive offerings.

One indicator of the growing amount of information available to consumers is the amount of spending on media. While this is true in many places around the world, it is particularly evident in the developed economies. U.S. household media spending, for example, is growing twice as fast as the economy, with the average expected to exceed $2000 per year by 2006, compared to some $1500 in 1996. And nearly 50 percent of the population will be members of "on-line households" by 2006.

Business customers are likewise becoming informationally empowered. Historically, business people wanting to keep abreast of business happenings around the globe waited for delivery of printed business periodicals. Even today, these print products remain a main source of business information. However, to meet business's insatiable appetite for faster and faster information, many publications now offer a "link" in many stories, allowing readers the opportunity to get more detailed information from the publication's website. Some providers offer paid subscriptions to electronic news services with in-depth business news available anytime, while other services offer an e-mail alert to breaking stories. Such media keep business-to-business markets alive with new product and service information from around the globe. It has empowered twenty-first century customers by keeping them instantly aware of all events critical to their interests. It is in the area of prices, however, that customer information empowerment has been felt most directly, particularly the globalization of pricing.

PRICES GO GLOBAL

In the past, many companies doing business around the world practiced *geographic pricing,* pricing the same product differently, depending on locale (beyond simple adjustments for shipping, tariffs, etc.). This geographic pricing was supported by the lack of knowledge consumers in higher-priced markets had about pricing in lower-priced markets. Since today, however, retail consumers and commercial customers have access to pricing information from around the world, companies are forced to establish *global prices.* In a commercial context, large global customers are demanding that their major suppliers treat them as *global accounts,* with consistent pricing and uniform service throughout the world. In many commercial areas, suppliers are forming global account teams to deal with global customers, and one of the early casualties is geographic pricing. Many suppliers, both large and small have reported huge growth in the number of accounts managed on a global basis.

In most businesses today, regional if not global pricing structures are emerging. In Europe, for example, Pan-European companies are demanding a "one price for Europe" bid for products that were formerly sold at a different price in each country. The introduction of an EU common currency, the Euro, should speed this process. It is only a matter of time until all pricing is global.

HARNESSING THE POWER OF GLOBAL INFORMATION

Information about pricing is just one facet of customer information empowerment. Customers now enjoy access to virtually every type of information about products and services. Savvy companies recognize that the microprocessor, in combination with software and digital technologies, has changed the whole idea of customer information—what it is, who controls it, how it can be used, shared, spent, or hoarded. These companies are not waiting for the customer to demand information. They are becoming proactive in sharing information about their companies, products, and services.

These proactive companies also recognize that information is more than mere number crunching and are sharing information with customers as a basis for common action. This tool applies to end-user consumers and channel intermediaries as well. Packaged goods companies Frito-Lay, Procter & Gamble, and Nabisco, for example, use hand-held computers to scan retail shelves. This tool instantly tracks consumer trends, speeds restocking, and provides valuable feedback to both the producer and their channel partners for coordinated action. The result is better service and cost savings that can be passed on to consumers.

Real customer focus is finally replacing product focus. The day of the passive consumer has vanished. If not willingly provided with the full information they want, customers go elsewhere with little hesitation. With competitive product information just a keystroke away on the Internet, customer switching costs are now near zero. Pushed by time and budget constraints and rallied by consumer "scares," such as recent concerns about silicone breast implants, the modern consumer actively seeks out new levels of product information.

When too pressed to get it all themselves, consumers are turning to reliable, independent, third-party sources, from consumer information consultants to a new breed of software known as Agents. These software agents, called *knowbots*, or knowledge robots, are just appearing on the scene, but they promise to become a major source of help for consumers to efficiently sort through the mass of available information. In recognition of the customer demand for information and advice, entrepreneurs are taking up the gauntlet and offering independent information on products and services from insurance to new cars and computers. A former auto salesperson, for example, saw the growing need for concrete, unbiased information among consumers bombarded by slick advertisements and conflicting data. For a fee, she removes much of the hassle of new-car purchasing by handling details about specific vehicles, including pricing comparisons, dealer and manufacturer incentives, and the actual purchasing negotiations.

Like an avalanche rumbling down a mountain, the push by consumers for fast, in-depth product information is gathering momentum. The desire of individuals and businesses to tap into available information sources can be measured by the increasing speed of adoption of new information networks. Cable television required 25 years to reach a critical mass of 10 million customers, but cell phones and VCRs took only 9 years to achieve that level. The World Wide Web, the ultimate source for consumer empowerment, reached the same plateau in a mere 5 years.

Today, no area of consumer or corporate activity is immune from the withering onslaught of network technologies—the most important of which is the Internet—that have opened everything from corporate financial information to radically different channels for consumer and commercial buying and selling and new levels of consumer access. Some products, such as those requiring custom fitting or a tactile response for purchase, will never be "sold" on the Internet. But the availability on the Net of in-depth product information will impact virtually every type of consumer and commercial transaction. The old "mushroom" principle of dealing with customers has given way to a whole new corporate strategic principle: Assume that the customer can, does, or will know as much as, if not more, than the supplier does!

ACTIVE ENGAGEMENT IN THE MARKET PROCESS

The second powerful notion about twenty-first century customers is that once informationally empowered, they seek active engagement in the market process. In effect, customers are demanding more and more involvement in every step of the process. Business theory has long held that the customer is at the front end of the process. But in practice, most companies put customers at the tail end. Often the first customers learn of a new product or service is when they are the recipients of a sales call or see an advertisement announcing something new. The staggering failure of almost three-quarters of all new products is testament to this fact. Such negligence is fading rapidly, however. Customers increasingly demand to be in the R&D labs, in the factories and the marketing departments, and on new product focus teams. Companies willing to pull customers "into the loop" find eager and helpful partners.

One particularly enlightening example of active engagement in the market process is health care. At one time, most patients were relatively passive. Some even submitted to surgery for reasons they didn't understand. Not today. Patients have forced the FDA to amend its procedures for the approval of new drugs. They've successfully lobbied the Centers for Disease Control and Congress to undertake research in new patient concerns. A major source of empowerment also comes from self-help groups—whose memberships now run to the millions—that assist patients in dealing with the intimidating health care system. These groups have created a new confidence among patients that ensures they can articulate what care they want and what kinds of care they will not accept. Even the relatively new "managed care" health service organizations have felt the power of the engaged consumer. When denied coverage for certain medical treatments, patients are increasingly taking to the courts to force the issue.

In addition to being the catalyst in creating empowered and demanding customers, technology is also frequently the key for companies to proactively engage customers in their new product development activities. Assume, for example, you need a new suit, fast, for an overseas business trip. No problem, according to retail clothing experts. Department stores are being equipped with computer-driven kiosks for customer selection of style, fabric, and color, and with optical body scanners for precise measurements. This information is relayed by satellite to a manufacturing plant and within days the suit is delivered. Personalized design of clothes is one of the fastest growing trends in the fashion industry, and this scenario is echoed in other industries. As customers increasingly gain the power to design their own clothes, for example, they will demand to participate directly in everything else the market has to offer.

CUSTOMERS SHAPE THE NEW PRODUCT DEVELOPMENT PROCESS

The new product development process is much too important to the twenty-first century customer to let producers do it alone. In fact, the companies that are now succeeding in the global village are those that have discovered how to make their customers partners early in the process. Like their customers, they're harnessing the power of information technology to get the specific information they need. However, the ability to understand technological, demographic, and market trends takes on a special urgency in a fast-paced global environment where information seldom, if ever, arrives in any orderly, linear pattern. In the real world, management is often bombarded on all sides by reports, computer-generated data, and rumor. New ways of thinking about and interpreting customer input are needed. But even chaotic systems exhibit patterns that can be discerned over time, and a number of smart companies are aggressively trying to learn *pattern recognition* as a means to understanding customer needs.

This ability to recognize patterns and move beyond the competition to provide timely, easy-to-use product information and services, thus getting early customer involvement in the process, is crucial to today's success. New interactive electronic media present companies with a vast array of marketing options and business challenges to marketers. Like the one-stop shopping convenience enjoyed by busy consumers who frequent megastores for everything from groceries to banking, eye exams to auto repairs, Internet services are offering shoppers one-stop "mega-stores" and "mega-indexes" to categorize sites and provide ease of movement from one site to the next.

Acxiom Corporation contributed to the potential for increased direct user control of marketing database resources through the introduction of Marketguide, a system which combines Windows-based PCs with the client/server database to provide easy access to marketing information. Through software services such as mapping, testing and application of scoring models, or querying and segmenting of the marketing database, they are providing rich new insights into customer needs. Such real time consumer feedback transforms traditional one-way mass marketing into a system in which marketers develop successful new products; craft ads; make channel, price, and place decisions; and measure results, all with a continuous customer dialogue.

Not all "get the customer into the process" activities require databases and electronic interaction. Some of the best are decidedly simple and personal. Some companies are using a new qualitative technique to get greater understanding of customer needs and greater levels of involvement. Known as "Day In the Life Of" or DILO research, it involves having multifunctional product teams spend a DILO with key customers. The research recognizes the importance of customers and enables managers and product teams to assess specific customer needs and interpret data in order to provide solutions. DILO research offers organizations an excellent opportunity to look, listen, and learn. For example, following DILO research, a shipping manager gains new perspective on the receiving department of a valued customer. Still others are *requiring* senior executives to spend a prescribed amount of time with customers.

Northern Telecom (now Nortel), when breaking into a market characterized by strongly held ties between Regional Bell Operating Companies (RBOCs) and traditional supplier AT&T, used a wide variety of customer involvement programs: customer councils and customer product/service steering groups; user groups for almost every product line; frequent seminars (not just focused on products, but industry "think" sessions as well) for all levels and functions within customer organizations;

and "president's roundtables," where the president and senior staff would meet routinely with their counterparts in customer organizations to discuss immediate issues and long-term product directions. One user group for the company's private telephone switching products even grew into an autonomous, global organization with an annual meeting, trade show, publications, and other communications programs.

PUTTING "CUSTOMER WINDOWS" IN THE R&D LAB AND THE FACTORY

The new customer listening posts just described are critically important, but real success comes from including the customer throughout the marketing process. Honda's active engagement of customers in the marketing process extends beyond traditional surveys and focus groups. Videotaped customer test-drives led to the discovery of how subtle changes could provide greater customer satisfaction. For example, parents making frequent fast-food runs suggested changes in the rear seat window so that food and drinks can be passed through to little leaguers and ballerinas with fewer spills.

Honda's efforts to extend customer involvement included an innovative program called "E.T. Phone Home." In effect, they put the customer in the factory. The goals were threefold: (1) Assess the level of customer satisfaction for the Honda Accord; (2) obtain customer feedback regarding future improvements; (3) increase customer loyalty by establishing ties between customers and the workers who build their cars. Over a 3-month period, Honda factory workers contacted over 47,000 Accord owners to see how they liked their new cars.

Global automakers are not alone in their desire to encourage closer ties and greater customer participation in their businesses. Baby product companies have traditionally encouraged parental involvement in product development and marketing. Managers of Gerber's Graduates baby food line, in addition to developing a strong advertising campaign and direct mailings, ventured into grass roots sampling and are now frequent visitors to parenting fairs and nursery schools to talk to new mothers.

Grass roots sampling is a long-established part of a marketing strategy called "customer visits." New research however has directly linked frequent customer contact, i.e., actual visits to customer sites, to the success rate of new products and services. This research has established a direct correlation between the intensity of relationships—between R&D, marketing, and customers—and market success.

From manufacturing to retailing, companies that recognize customer empowerment and respond by getting customer involvement in their business processes are the big winners. The development during the 1980s and 1990s of the superstore phenomenon is one of the best examples of responses to new retail demands. Sam's, Toys R Us, CompUSA, and Home Depot demonstrated the phenomenal rewards to be had by getting the customer engaged in the process. Wal-Mart CEO David Glass considers Home Depot, which is a benchmark in customer engagement, the "best run organization in America today." Home Depot's successful strategy to get the do-it-yourself customer intimately involved is not just a U.S. phenomenon; it's finding success around the world, in countries as diverse as Mexico and Israel.

Such companies achieve success and gain reputations for customer loyalty by encouraging customers to become actively engaged in the company. They recognize that in today's world of business, the customer is an active partner in the success of the firm.

THE ONLY FIVE THINGS CUSTOMERS WANT

Being "market driven," "listening to the customer," "putting the customer first," and all such slogans have long been mantras in business. The only problem is that few organizations actually did it. Customer information systems were often too slow, and the information gaps between R&D, manufacturing, and marketing within companies were too wide to consistently develop and deliver what the customer wanted. Consumers got used to settling for what would do rather than exactly what they needed and wanted.

Today's customer is knowledgeable, engaged, and powerful. The twenty-first century customer wants just five things: speed, quality, variety, service, and price. With a plethora of information and a world full of competitors just a keystroke away on the Internet, they demand these things and they will get them. For businesses, it is a challenging list, but organizations that can consistently deliver on them are experiencing great competitive success.

Obviously, this list suggests that customers have become very demanding, but that's a positive thing. Demanding customers create enormous opportunities and, ultimately, great companies.

TWENTY-FIRST CENTURY CUSTOMERS DEMAND INSTANT GRATIFICATION

In a recent United Airlines television commercial, managers are kept waiting for the start of a meeting. By the time a company executive enters the room, the managers are fuming over the waste of their valuable time. The executive acknowledges the managers' feelings of anger and admonishes them to remember this moment when dealing with passengers.

In today's "too little time, too much to do" climate, consumers increasingly see *instant gratification* as an inalienable right (not far behind the right to free speech). Consumers around the world, for example, demand quick, one-stop grocery shopping at huge superstores and fast-food emporiums. If the supermarket houses a bank, an auto repair center, and a video store, so much the better. Fast, one-stop multiple-use retail and service outlets are catching on too. Many new gas stations now include fast-food restaurants to ease time demands for customers. And it's not unusual for giant superstores like Wal-Mart to offer tire centers, video rentals, fast-food outlets, banks, beauty parlors, travel agents, eyewear, and car repair as integral parts of the store. A TV commercial for BP gives us a glimpse of how far this could go. A roving gas truck allows a car to drive aboard while en route, fill up the tank and get something to eat, all while the truck continues down the road.

Legions of consumers everywhere opt for the burger chain drive-thru or the local restaurant that touts "express lunches in 5 minutes or less." They click buttons to access everything from instant cash and banking information at ATMs to 50+ channels of entertainment on cable, not to mention the instant information available on the Internet. A five-minute wait in line can seem almost unbearable.

At first, computers seemed lightning fast. Now, however, growing numbers of users can't tolerate even the few seconds that computers take to boot. Millisecond "boot time" has become a competitive differentiation between PCs. Perhaps most telling of all is the global growth of home shopping networks on TV; they demonstrate that people not only want it fast, they don't even want to leave home to get it.

Consequently, today's successful companies are developing innovative ways to respond to this desire for instant gratification. Notwithstanding the advertising fantasy of mobile gas stations, oil companies are indeed speeding customers through the station with the pay-at-the-pump credit card feature. Customers can fill up quickly with no human intervention, no cash register, no lines. Rental car companies are using a host of new technologies to speed customers ever faster into and out of their lots. Banks are grabbing corners of supermarkets to provide fast access to cash. Hotels are providing in-house booking facilities for departing airline passengers to help reduce airport waiting time.

But it's not just in food, computers, banks, and gas stations that consumers are demanding ever-faster service. Many homebuyers, for example, are demanding faster and faster methods of house hunting, despite it often being the most expensive purchase of a lifetime. To meet this need for speed, realtors offer computerized house shopping services and allow customers to quickly view homes via prerecorded videos of sale properties. Other realtors have placed computer kiosks in shopping malls, allowing convenient in-mall house shopping. And Internet services are quickly replacing the old paper multiple listings system (MLS) as new technologies allow customers to key in price, location, and other criteria and then electronically view potential purchases anywhere in the country. Even mortgages are available faster from Internet banks such as Canada's mbanx, which boasts an average mortgage approval time of 10 minutes.

Today, improvement in response time—whether to customer product and service demands or to customer complaints—is *the* critical key to success. Companies oriented to speed frequently track response times throughout the entire customer interaction process to eliminate bottlenecks. Meeting customer demands for instant gratification by improving cycle time requires flexibility and innovativeness.

The same focus on speed in consumer markets is found in commercial markets as well. One major bank found that the number-one criterion underlying relationships with commercial banking customers is speed—the faster the better. To achieve both speed to market and speed to volume, industrial companies are using new tools with dramatic results. One company decided that for their twenty-first century customers, instant gratification just wasn't soon enough. So California-based Cyber-Source now sells and distributes software via the Internet. Customers order on-line but then have the option of regular or Internet deliver. Internet delivery is practical primarily for commercial customers with high-speed networks, but the potential for such services for noncommercial consumers is coming quickly. When it does, virtually everyone will demand a customer-supplier relationship based on instant gratification.

TWENTY-FIRST CENTURY CUSTOMERS DEMAND GLOBAL BEST QUALITY

For nearly 50 years, W. Edwards Deming and J. M. Juran, the masterminds of industrial quality, dominated corporate thinking in Japan. With their passionate focus on quality, the Japanese were able to push aside manufacturers around the world who had, for too long, taken their customers for granted. In the United States, the automobile and electronics industries felt the greatest impact from Japanese competitors. To fight back, by the mid-1980s, virtually every company worldwide was chasing Japanese standards of quality. By that time, however, the Japanese had grabbed large chunks of the global market and were creating shock waves for companies everywhere. And they were quick to move beyond *atarimae hinshitsu* (quality that is expected) to *miryokuteki hinshitsu* (quality that fascinates).

Today, almost every company in every country has scrambled aboard the quality bandwagon. Companies worldwide instituted quality teams and reinforced employee and public awareness of high quality standards. One company, wanting to drive home the quality message, even renamed streets and access roads leading to its manufacturing plants using some form of the word quality.

The quality message is perhaps the most enduring in the past 50 years of corporate history. And all the quality rhetoric has had a lasting impact on consumers, with some perceptions hard to overcome. Many American consumers, despite the equal or sometimes superior quality of U.S. products, give a higher rating to Japanese products. In a classic example, Mitsubishi, in a joint venture with Chrysler Corporation, began production of *identical* automobiles; the only difference was the nameplate—the Mitsubishi "Eclipse" and the Plymouth "Laser." However, when these cars hit the market, Chrysler sold a paltry 14 Lasers per dealership, while Mitsubishi averaged 100 per dealership. When American consumers were asked why they preferred the Eclipse, they replied that the Japanese make better quality cars.

This incident reflects many of the reasons for the quality focus in American industry throughout the 1980s and early 1990s. The overwhelming attention to quality, TQM, quality circles, and other strategies led to the creation of the Malcolm Baldrige National Quality Award in 1988, mimicking Japan's Deming Award, a long-standing and much coveted honor. American companies in the '80s and '90s spent literally billions of dollars to improve quality and vie for the award. In the early nineties winning the Baldrige assured great admiration and press coverage. One commentator at the time even noted that printing Baldrige award applications had become the biggest business in Washington, D.C.

THE GLOBALIZATION OF QUALITY

While the Baldrige and Deming awards remain of genuine interest in their respective countries, the globalization of quality has eclipsed their importance. An increasing number of businesses around the world are now obtaining certification in ISO 9000, QS-9000, and ISO 14001 (environmental standards). Created by the International Standards Organization in Geneva, Switzerland, certification in these crucial areas provides greater compatibility of components, as well as standardization of processes, packaging, inspection and testing, measurements, documentation, delivery, records, internal audits, environmental control, disposal procedures, etc. So pervasive has ISO certification become that companies as diverse as soft drink bottlers, banks, and even television networks have all been awarded ISO certification. ISO certification involves a long, complicated process, and some critics argue that it assures only consistent processes, not quality products and services. However, as large global companies achieve ISO certification and demand the same of all their local suppliers, the world's consumers are being provided with a global benchmark and assurance of quality and environmental responsibility.

While consumers around the world continue to think of quality in different ways (e.g., in Japan it's equated with *product durability*; in the United States with *design intent*; in the European Union with *repairability*), quality has clearly taken on a global dimension.

Unfortunately, in the blind rush to follow the standardized prescriptions of quality gurus, many companies failed to include customers in their programs. They fell into the trap of believing that a quality product is synonymous with customer satisfaction, and it's not. Even those companies that stand as benchmarks for quality can provide useful lessons in what not to do in pursuing quality over customer requirements.

CUSTOMER-DEFINED QUALITY

The best example comes from Florida Power and Light (FP&L), a quality leader throughout the world since 1989, when it became the first American company to capture the Deming Award. However, in its total focus on quality and strict adherence to meeting specific quality standards, the company discovered mounting problems in a number of areas. Attention to customer needs suffered as customer service line representatives hurried callers in order to achieve a quality standard for speed (answering 85 percent of all calls within 45 seconds). But the response to any problem, from service installation to moving a filing cabinet in the office, fell under an analysis process that included seven steps and tracking 41 indicators. The process itself became a headache. Without abandoning quality, FP&L revised its strict standards, reduced its 41 indicators to 3, and allowed employees the freedom to solve problems in innovative ways without the fear of leaving out some arbitrary step. Today, even Xerox, a company that reversed its downward spiral by adopting new quality initiatives—and winning a Baldrige award in the process in an intense fight with Japanese competitors—now prefers the use of metrics for customer requirement and results over a strict focus on product quality.

Hard goods companies are not alone in rethinking quality. Service companies are refocusing on both the cost and value of quality. But unlike standardized manufacturing, the characteristics of service industries determine the unique requirements for customer-defined quality.

Letting customers define quality in service organizations is being matched by a renewed focus on customers by manufacturing industries. Hewlett-Packard's new "Quality One on One" campaign, for example, approaches quality from the customer's viewpoint and makes it complementary to its own perspective. This combination meets the optimum standards in service quality by allowing the customer to drive the quality process, therefore clearly defining expectations of what *should* happen.

In the shape of things today, successful quality efforts require top management to make meeting and exceeding customer satisfaction, of which product and service quality are a part, but only a part, a priority of company strategy. They need also to communicate that message widely and give everyone in the organization the necessary training and support to meet those goals. Today's quality leadership begins with an intimate knowledge of how customers define satisfaction and product or service quality and an emphasis on results in meeting and exceeding customer expectations, as opposed to rigid product quality processes. The key element here is customer expectation, often missed in the application of earlier standardized quality approaches.

TWENTY-FIRST CENTURY CUSTOMERS DEMAND EVERYTHING CUSTOMIZED TO THEIR NEEDS

Ken Baker, vice president of research and development at GM, envisions the day when customers will enter a dealer's "virtual ordering station" and design a car to personal specifications—color, trim, instrument panel, layout, sound system, handling characteristics, even upholstery fabric woven to a personal design. Baker likes to describe how the order is then relayed immediately to manufacturing, which notifies suppliers and schedules assembly for the following day. By the end of the second day the finished product is loaded for delivery, and on the third day, another satisfied customer drives a customized vehicle off the dealer lot. While much of the technology described by Baker is available today, the rest is not too far in the future. GM's Inland Fisher Guide division has already developed a computer-driven knitting process capable of reproducing interior photos and artwork. Baker says GM's goal is to be able to produce an economic lot size of one, using reprogrammable, general-purpose tooling in small assembly plants.

Automakers are not alone, as a host of companies are customizing their products and services to meet this customer demand for variety. Custom bicycle maker Panasonic uses its Panasonic Individual Custom Systems (PICS) to offer bicycles in 11,655 combinations, including customer selection of paint scheme, color, measurements, and accessories. In addition to product customization, Panasonic offers speed of delivery (three weeks or less) and prices at the same level as its competitors' semicustom bicycles. Custom publishing, the creation of unique publications for individual consumers, is one of the strongest undercurrents in publishing today.

Customization is becoming increasingly recognized as a catalyst in customer loyalty, and by using advanced customer information systems and computerized manufacturing, companies today can effectively market to segments of one. As described in Chapter 2, advanced networking, computer technology, and robotics create unlimited potential for product customization in a number of industries and may herald a new era of craftsmanship. While underdeveloped countries corner the market for mass producing clothing, for instance, companies in the West may someday utilize new technology in small plants to focus on customized fashion. Innovative companies on the lookout for such customized product and service opportunities are moving to the forefront of their respective industries. It's important to remember, then, that today's empowered consumer has a new mantra, "I want it my way, or I don't want it at all!" The only acceptable company response is, "Give it to them their way, or don't bother."

TWENTY-FIRST CENTURY CUSTOMERS DEMAND PREEMPTIVE SERVICE

Listening to the demands of customers and responding to them in a timely fashion has always been the essence of customer service. The shape of today's business, however, increasingly requires *preemptive* customer service, service designed and delivered before the customer's point of requirement. It begins with understanding customer needs, and that comes only through in-depth interaction with customers.

Capturing customer information can be achieved in any number of traditional ways—point of sale and service questionnaires, follow-up interviews, warranty application forms, and many others, most of which have become routine. Increasingly, however, technology is offering new ways to obtain customer information, via bar coding and customer data warehouses, for example.

Many of today's businesses still think of customer service only in terms of accountability or *response* to problems. Smart companies understand that the shape of customer service today also entails *anticipation* and early delivery of solutions to customer problems and needs. Both anticipation of and response to customer service needs can be met only through advanced information and intense employee training.

The precise nature of preemptive customer service will, of course, vary with the nature of the business. Megastores such

as Home Depot and Lowe's stress competency, product famil-
iarity, and the ability to explain the "how to" aspects of products
to do-it-yourselfers. It can also mean competency, promptness,
flexibility, empathy, trustworthiness, reliability, and exceeding
obligations and customer expectations.

PREEMPTIVE SERVICE FROM PEOPLESOFT, INC.

While a number of companies seem to have recently "discovered"
service, some have been obsessed with it from their inception. And
in many cases their success in terms of customer acceptance and
financial performance has been quite dramatic. A case in point is
PeopleSoft, founded in 1987, and located in Pleasanton,
California. PeopleSoft chief executive, Dave Duffield, created an
organization to meet the special needs of companies that use
extensive outsourcing and require all their suppliers to work in
concert to reach collective goals. To meet the unique and constantly changing business problems of these companies, PeopleSoft
designed thousands of software packages to assist in the performance of daily coordination of human resources, logistics, production planning, and accounting. PeopleSoft products were designed
to be learned quickly and to help workers make informed decisions, while remaining flexible in response to change.

Of the 2500 employees at PeopleSoft, a staggering 40 percent
are devoted to customer service in the areas of account management, product support, and professional, education, and communication services. For many traditional organizations, such a
commitment to service seems extraordinary, but the numbers tell
the story. In competition with software giants such as Oracle and
SAP, PeopleSoft's 1996 earnings were over $55 million on rev-
enues of $430 million, up 89 percent over the previous year.
PeopleSoft stock appreciated nearly 720 percent over a two-year
period. The company anticipates revenues will double by the year
2000. It ranked 20th in a 1998 survey of the 100 Best
Companies to work for in America.

Their software programs serve over 1300 customers in a wide
variety of industries. Duffield values his employees and makes
sure each individual feels important to the success of PeopleSoft
and to its customers. To that end, he ignores the traditional trap-

pings of management. Duffield personally embodies the service ethic: working from a cubicle, answering his own phone calls and mail, and making sure his organization remains a fun place to work. Equally important, he ensures that the real power of the organization is on the front lines, service employees who deal directly with customers and their problems. Every employee is encouraged to develop strong working relationships with clients and is empowered to use discretionary funds to meet the needs of a specific client. Awards for outstanding customer service are given annually and include either cash or stock options. With stock returns running 115 percent annually since 1992, employees work hard for the opportunity to win these exceptional awards.

The lessons from PeopleSoft are obvious: Anticipate the future needs of customers; give employees and customers the tools they need to succeed; and flood the marketplace with experienced, service-oriented professionals. The result is a phenomenal success and a sterling reputation for service leadership.

One of the primary objectives of preemptive customer service efforts is to retain customers. Too many companies spend so much of their time trying to attract new customers that they overlook the obvious: Customer retention is the key to prolonged success. Hence the oft-cited statistic: It costs five times more to find a new customer than to retain an existing one.

TWENTY-FIRST CENTURY CUSTOMERS DEMAND THE GLOBAL BEST PRICE

The principal lesson of the Japanese invasion of U.S. consumer electronic and automobile markets in the 1970s was that the combination of world-class quality and global best price could dislodge even the most entrenched competitor.

A big corporate name is no longer a guarantee of success, and brand loyalty among consumers can be fleeting. Therefore focusing on value, the superior and continuing combination of quality and price, is what separates the winners from losers.

In recent years brand loyalty among customers spawned an enormous number of "customer frequency" marketing programs, generically patterned after airline frequent flyer programs. Intended to engender repeat business among top customers of a particular product or service, these programs often backfire on their sponsors unless great care is taken during the planning stages. In their initial enthusiasm to reward loyalty, many companies erred by latching on to overused ideas, underestimating program costs or overestimating customer use, offering extravagant incentives, or focusing on winning back customers while ignoring *why* the customer abandoned one brand for another. The bargaining war for customers is obvious in many industries; long distance phone service, for example, and the thrust of many programs is to encourage customers to chase after deals rather than establish a long-term relationship with one provider. Companies implementing frequency marketing programs must recognize the difference between "repeat business" and "loyalty," and provide incentives that focus on customer needs.

Unfortunately, market success often creates a comfort zone that encourages price inflation and a relaxing of quality standards, as a number of big-name companies have found. Computer giants like Compaq Computer are likewise focusing on value, introducing lower-priced but high-quality subbrands to complement major lines and attract new customers. Their innovative product lines are finding new distribution outlets in major retail locations such as Sears and warehouse superstores, attracting many first-time PC shoppers who shy away from the more intimidating computer or electronic stores.

A high-quality, low-price value strategy often enables smaller companies to take on industry giants. For example, a value pricing strategy combined with new technology advances (and, in fairness, a strong dollar) allowed Fuji Photo Film USA to improve its market share relative to the 35mm film leader, Kodak. Among supermarket and drugstore retailers, Fuji film sales have jumped dramatically. Evidence of Fuji's growth appeared in a 1997 television news story about Kodak layoffs. While filming Kodak's announcement about declining film sales, the television newscaster queried a large contingent of news photographers about their choice of film. The overwhelming majority flashed Fuji film boxes. The reason they gave: excellent quality and lower price.

The combination of customer empowerment, political conditions, and global competition in markets such as health care has led pharmaceutical companies to a reemphasis on value. Long accustomed to selling high quality, proprietary drugs for virtually any price they wished, drug companies are now using value pricing to gain competitive advantage in an increasingly difficult market.

In the United States, the sustained push for lower health care costs has placed new emphasis on pharmaceutical costs. The appeal of discounting through generics and the competition for lower prices among managed care groups forced pharmaceutical companies to reassess the impact of market forces and create new pricing strategies while maintaining top quality products. The scramble among big purchasers—hospitals, HMOs—to find the best value for customers increases what the industry has dubbed "managed competition." Drug companies that offer the best prices to HMOs, for example, can literally corner the market in a specific line of drugs.

In the establishment of customer value, perhaps no company exceeds Wal-Mart and its innovative policy of "brand name products at the guaranteed lowest price." Wal-Mart rewrote the rules of engagement in retail pricing. Companies in many other markets who seek to disrupt a long-standing competitive landscape with a new customer value proposition are mimicking Wal-Mart's approach. "We've been Wal-Marted!" is the new cry of despair heard from sluggish competitors who don't understand the value demands of today's informationally empowered and engaged customer.

Whether such strategies will prove successful remains to be seen. But these efforts and others like them indicate the seriousness with which companies in all industries are recognizing the importance of value to customers. The pace at which global market dynamics are changing, coupled with the growing information empowerment of consumers, translates into a global best-quality/global best-price value requirement for success in the global village.

MARKETING IN THE GLOBAL VILLAGE

Most of the dominant social, political, and economic paradigms of the past fifty years have completely disappeared or are rapidly heading that way. In politics, for example, regional communist regimes disintegrated into dozens of new democratic countries, and long-standing power bases such as Japan's LDP and Mexico's PRI, formerly one-party monopolies over otherwise democratic systems, are yielding to new centers of power. In business, both goods and services industries have experienced a major paradigm shift from producers to consumers as technology has put increased levels of information into the hands of consumers and empowered their new role as the prime movers in today's economy. As a result, marketing in the global village has emerged as a dominant new paradigm for business today. It has several important dimensions: Consumers have assumed power from producers; products must meet exacting new standards; and distribution times and prices are approaching zero.

POWERSHIFT: FROM PRODUCERS TO CONSUMERS

Until the emergence of the global village, producers held all the power in the marketplace. A frequently cited example of this comes from retail, where big national producers "dictated" shelf space to local or regional retailers. These large producers controlled the shelf because they knew (or said they knew) what consumers across the nation wanted. In today's world of retail, however, consumers stand at the center of power. With bar coding and sophisticated checkout terminals, retailers have real-time inventory and information systems that let them know instantly what's selling. Now retailers tell the producers what goes on the shelf. In reality, though, it's consumers who are dictating to the retailers exactly what they want, also in real time, and in a most direct way (with every dollar spent). In no uncertain terms, then, consumers now dictate shelf space, and they dictate the terms of every other product and service sold today, even in areas where "producers" have long clung to unchallenged power.

Just like retailers and consumer goods producers, physicians, pharmaceutical manufacturers, and other health-care providers are discovering that U.S. health-care consumers have changed drastically in the past few years. Informationally empowered consumers no longer go along automatically with whatever doctors or pharmaceutical companies tell them. Today's savvy health service customer has access to in-depth information from authoritative sources around the world and is increasingly likely to question health care providers about drugs and treatments. Once physician-driven, the market for health care and prescription drugs is now influenced by many other sources. Patients and payers now exert a major influence on drug prices, insurance reimbursement, and treatment selection. Even given the fractious nature of the health-care debate in the United States, one principle has remained sacrosanct, individual choice.

In most markets, the demand for a direct relationship between producers and consumers becomes more and more intense, and the channels of distribution become shorter and shorter as consumers gain power. Everywhere around the world, wholesalers, distributors, and dealers (some industries in the past had as many as three, four, or more channel members) are getting squeezed out of the distribution chain because they are little more than aggregators; they don't add any real value to the process. In fact, today, the direct pull between producer and consumer is so strong that any distributor not adding real consumer value is getting squeezed out of the channel. The sophisticated logistics and communication technologies described in Part 1 are permitting producers and customers direct, fast, and efficient communication and distribution linkages that meet the increasing customer demand for specifying product design and features, shorter delivery times, and value-added information and services.

The more sophisticated and demanding customers become, regardless of where in the world they're located, and the more evolved technologies become that allow savvy producers to meet the need, the more corporate strategy shifts from a product focus to customer focus. The challenge for business is to understand and respond to customer demands by tailoring a product or a service to these requirements and find innovative ways to streamline the entire customer value process. Wal-Mart, one of the most successful retailers in history, increasingly bypasses wholesalers and distributors to deal directly with producers. The company's success is credited to knowing what customers want and when they want it. To beat the competition, Wal-Mart establishes direct, fast, and efficient connections to producers. Middlepeople who slow the process and add costs are eliminated.

A major reason for the new urgency in addressing the producer-to-customer powershift is the lack of brand loyalty. In their search for value, consumers today show a greater propensity to switch products, stores, or service distribution networks to get what they want. This new reality affects service companies as well as hard goods product companies. Banks, brokerage houses, and real estate organizations are really distributors positioned between those who have money to lend or stocks or property to sell and those who wish to borrow, invest, or buy. The survival of such entities depends on their ability to find and provide real value to consumers who increasingly have the option to go directly to the source of value. And increasingly, that real value is information-based.

This powershift from producer to customer is also evident in the distribution of commercial products. Technology and global competition in all phases of transport has led to customers expecting and getting all types of new services unavailable a few years ago. It has forced traditional transportation suppliers to create more value with a whole new range of services, from managing a customer's global distribution to designing customized shipping boxes. Customer demand also spurs other service upgrades, like paperwork. Major shipping competitors now provide a simplified single bill for shipping on several modes of transport to points worldwide.

There is one overriding consequence to this producer to consumer powershift. Customers now truly hold the balance of power in the marketplace. The manifestation of that can be best understood in the strategic shift from focus on markets, to focus on customers. Although this chapter is entitled "Marketing in the Global Village," in today's world of business, there are no markets anymore, only individual customers. Therefore, survival in today's environment requires recognition that twentieth-century concepts of markets and marketing are no longer viable.

An excellent example of this reality can be found in what some companies are calling "customer value genetics." This new approach does not treat customers as a group. It attempts with each individual commercial customer to establish joint common values as a basis of supplier-customer behavior, and it provides a framework and rules for joint relationship management. It recognizes that customers often redefine their values and needs and that the supplier should change in concert with the customer (hence "genetics"). This concept mandates each individual customer, not market segment, as the driving force within the organization.

Unfortunately, no term easily replaces the word "marketing." Thus, markets and marketing remain the terms of the day and of this book.

NO MARKETS...ONLY CUSTOMERS

A brief overview of the evolution of marketing will aid in understanding how customers replaced markets in corporate strategy. Exhibit 6.1 presents an overview of this evolution. In reviewing

	Mass Marketing	Consumer Marketing	Relationship Marketing	Global Marketing	Intimacy Marketing
Time frame	1950s	1960s	1970s	1980s	1990s
Focus	Product	Consumer	External environment	Global environment	Customer intimacy
Objective	Profit	Market share	Stakeholder benefits	Global market share	Exceeding customer expectations
Action	Sales	Marketing (4 Ps)	Relationship management	Sustainable competitive advantage	Customer engagement
Audience	Mass	Segments	Niches	Clusters	Individual

NOTE: Adapted from Varki, Sajev, and Roland T. Rust, "Technology and Optimal Segment Size," *Marketing Letters*, 9(2), 1998, 147–167.

EXHIBIT 6.1 Marketing in the Global Village.

this exhibit, keep in mind that many of the features of a particular phase of marketing do not disappear, but are subsumed in the next phase. For example, the focus on market share in the consumer phase of marketing did not disappear as a relevant metric in the evolution to relationship phase. It simply became one part of a larger set of concerns or approaches.

Mass marketing, the beginning of a business function.   The concept of marketing is literally hundreds of years old and is attributed by some scholars to early efforts in Japan to formally organize buyers and sellers. Modern marketing came about just prior to World War II, but it essentially took hold in the postwar economy when supply was scarce and consumer confidence and purchasing power was growing rapidly. This early period is often referred to as the era of mass or product marketing. During this time, the ability to manufacture and physically distribute a product was often all that was needed for success. Consumers were hungry for all goods, they had money to spend, and if anything, marketing was essentially a product development function. Sales professionals within an organization were the closest to anything resembling marketing activities.

During this phase, businesses did little in the way of differentiating their products, and the individual consumer was thought to be but one of a huge mass of consumers, all of whom, it was believed, wanted identical products and services. This phenomenon was often referred to as "keeping up with the Joneses." In the telephone industry, for example, everyone got the same black rotary phone. Marketing's big job was to ensure national distribution and presence. Scorekeeping was typically a straight profit calculation, and advertising consisted of getting a single message to a mass audience via the rapidly evolving mass media.

Consumers make their presence felt.   In the mid to late 1950s, academics and practitioners began to notice that not everyone was interested in identical goods and services and that there was money to be made by thinking about more segregated sets of consumer needs. Also about this time, select individuals, usually recruited out of sales organizations, began appearing in headquarters' offices with the title of marketing attached. Market research began to take hold as an important part of the process. The core concepts of market *segments*, large subgroups within the population wanting unique products and services, along with the *4 Ps* (product, price, promotion, and place of distribution) were put into practice. Scorekeeping also became more sophisticated, and calculations such as *return on sales* (ROS) and *market share* were added to those of profits as essential tools for managing the business.

Stakeholders "stake" their claims and marketers discover customer relationships. Marketing concepts from the 1950s and 1960s were all subsumed in the further evolution of the paradigm during the late 1960s and early 1970s, as societal changes and "oil shocks" reminded managers that other constituencies, or stakeholders, required attention, e.g., governments, employees, environmentalists, Nader's Raiders, etc. Marketing and business success now was seen to be concerned with the entire external environment, because generating *stake*holder as well as *stock*holder benefits were critical if a business was going to succeed, and in some cases, even allowed to exist. Unfortunately for some producers, customers were being lured away by companies willing to aim their products and services at smaller and smaller segments that came to be known as *niches*. Reaching those customer niches was becoming easier as the mass media began to fragment into specialized media vehicles aimed at increasing smaller and more narrowly defined audiences.

Growing consumer power and increasingly sophisticated and cheaper technologies arrived on the scene about the same time. This "coincidence" created the next evolutionary step in marketing, relationship marketing. Some, particularly in consumer and direct marketing businesses, refer to it as database marketing. Whatever it's called, this type of marketing focuses on the development of a closer attachment between companies (whether automakers, retailers, or rock groups) and their consumers. In contrast to simply targeting customer segments, relationship building required development over time and attention to personal customer needs.

Service companies also realized the need for customer relationships. Leading insurance companies, for example, recognized the main ingredient for success was the need to specialize and develop relationships with narrow market segments. Realizing they could no longer compete effectively over the long term by attempting to be all things to all people, they began to profile clients individually and establish prices on the basis of the value of the long-term customer relationship.

Marketing goes global. Many countries, such as the Netherlands, Finland, Hong Kong, and Canada, have long relied on international trade for a significant portion of their GNP. But the true globalization of markets—for all producers and most countries—began in earnest in the late 1960s and early 1970s. All of a sudden, businesses were no longer competing in a domestic market, but a global one. For many companies, the new scorekeeping was simple: *survival* in the face of fast, aggressive, global competitors. The most nimble companies recognized early on that their global market share was the key metric for measuring success. The marketer's attention was now focused more broadly. Instead of simply manipulating the marketing mix and making sure all stakeholder interests were addressed, the marketer had to engage all those within the organization to create and exploit a *sustainable* competitive advantage, i.e., one that is constantly evolving and improving. "Going global" promised enormous rewards, but the competition was fierce and unrelenting. In addition, new technologies in manufacturing, information, and logistics were making it increasingly easy to produce and deliver goods and services tailored to smaller and smaller segments called *clusters*. "Think Global, Act Local" became the rallying cry for many companies trying to satisfy the needs of both global markets and local customers. Markets, it seemed, were growing bigger (global) and smaller (into clusters) at the same time, one of those logical inconsistencies of the global village.

The marketing realities of the 1980s, however, were all subsumed in the 1990s into the next evolutionary phase of marketing. Although no "catch name" for today's marketing has

achieved universal acceptance among scholars and practitioners, for the purposes of this book at least, it's referred to as *intimacy marketing*.

Intimacy marketing. At the beginning of the 1990s, the unex-
pectedly early (and harsh) arrival of the twenty-first century—
with its growing economic difficulties, sophisticated and
informed consumers, and intensified global competition—forced
yet another evolution in the approach to marketing. In intimacy
marketing, success lies with the producer who can effectively and
efficiently integrate the individual customer into the process of
creating and delivering the exact product or service desired. The
objective is to develop a situation in which the sale is the culmination of a long process of engaging the customer into significant
parts of the business. Concepts of mass, segments, and clusters
of customers have given way to the ultimate segment of one. The
marketer's key strategic weapon has become the understanding
of an individual customer's expectations and attempting not just
to satisfy them, but to exceed them. In industrial and commercial
markets, creating customer intimacy can involve the entire supply or value system, essentially integrated and organized by end
customer needs. Such engagement is already taking place in a
number of industries—retail, automobile, banking, electronics,
and health care, to name a few, and many are being forced by customers or global economics.

SMARTER, BETTER, CHEAPER, FASTER, SMALLER, AND MORE ELEGANT PRODUCTS AND SERVICES

The second dimension of marketing in the global village presents
a unique and unrelenting problem for every marketer. Free falling
computer chip prices, the corresponding escalation of chip functionality, and the availability of global products with world-class
design have convinced the twenty-first century customer to
expect that in the global village, virtually every product should be
smarter, better, cheaper, faster, smaller, and more elegant.

Smarter. Consumers are already familiar with rudimentary "smart" products: the coffeemaker that starts moments before you arise, the steam iron or space heater that automatically turns itself off after a certain period, or the automobile that starts from a remote switch and shuts off its own lights. But today's consumer demands more information, more functionality, more of everything. In response, inexpensive microchips are finding their way into a whole class of goods, from toys and consumer durables to cars and homes. Products are becoming more information intensive. Margins on new products increase as information content is increased, so even some established products are being revitalized by the addition of information content. Extremely low-priced but high-function computer chips are migrating into credit cards, car dashboards, and even the "dumbest" of appliances, the TV. Microsoft's WebTV, for example, uses a $15 chip that is a high-speed data modem, computes 200 million transactions per second, and processes high-quality video.

Innovative applications of intelligence embedded into goods and services provide organizations of all types with a means of securing and maintaining market leadership. Kroger introduced hand-held bar-code scanners that allow customers to scan product prices as they fill their grocery carts, keeping track of their expenditures and saving time in the checkout line. (It also provides the stores and suppliers with up-to-the-minute inventory data!) FedEx leapt ahead of competitors in the development of smart packages, actually a whole high-tech tracking system with everything from bar-coding and laser-scanner computers to software packages that allow customers to label and track their own shipments. Customers can even check package status through the Internet. The system permits them to tap into FedEx computer systems. Being smarter doesn't always require a sophisticated technology solution, as Oral B demonstrated with their simple "blue strip" toothbrush that alerts the user when it's time for a new brush. What these companies learned, whether with advanced technology or simple blue stripes, is that today's truly successful product or service provides consumers with increasing information content. Smarter is the standard for today's new products.

Better. Innovative companies are looking at ways to make even the most common of products better. For example, CEO Peter Redford, of TV Interactive, became enthralled with the crude technology that allowed children's books to provide push-button sound. To advance this concept, his company improved on traditional paper by creating "smart" paper that reacts to touch. Using this technology, a consumer can test the latest CD without taking off the wrapper or access a block of text in a how-to book. By pressing a spot on the smart paper, the user signals an embedded microchip that releases audio or video onto the computer screen. Companies are engineering an astonishing number of improvements for better products and services, including "hot badges" (wearable computers) and pagers that receive brief voice messages without the aid of a telephone. However, as in the case of "smarter," better does not always mean high-tech gadgetry. Commonplace items, such as bathtubs with water-sealed doors that allow older or disabled people to enter without climbing over the side; automobiles and minivans featuring in-seat child safety restraints; batteries in packages with energy-testing devices; and wiper blades that won't stick to the windshield in freezing weather—all are examples of simple but innovative ideas to make products better. Services too need to be better, only here, better usually means error free. Errors are the number-one consumer complaint in most service businesses—a mistake in a financial transaction, an order shipped incomplete, incorrect information from a service representative, you name it. So smart service operators are building error-free, zero-tolerance programs into their service delivery strategies, because a mistake often chases away a customer forever.

Cheaper. The word *cheaper* conjures up images of giant discounters and wholesalers, as well as everyday, low-price (EDLP) strategies. But companies in virtually every business are finding innovative ways to design, manufacture, and market increasingly cheaper (or higher value) products. Efforts include forming alliances or partnering with other companies in order to speed design efforts, implementing CAD technologies in order to reduce costly prototyping of new products, and restructuring processes in order to cut out costly steps or middlemen. The Customer Sales Center at Sun Microsystems lives by the motto, cheaper, faster, better. Toward that goal, the company has insisted that all suppliers install electronic data interchange (EDI) in order to improve service to high-dollar, high-transaction-volume customers.

AUTOMATION PUSHES CAR TIRE PRICES TOWARD ZERO

Several years ago a group of MBA students traveled to Japan and toured the head office of a major global tire manufacturer. Following a presentation on the company's hiring procedures for college engineers, a student asked, "What's the procedure for hiring a factory worker?"

"I'm sorry, but we can't tell you," the official responded.

"But why can't you tell me?" the student pressed.

"The reason is that we can't remember. We haven't hired a factory worker in almost twenty years."

The official went on to explain that the company goal was to have every step in the production of a tire so automated that no human hand touched the tire from start to finish. Such goals are not unique to Japan, however. The goal of total automation is quickly becoming a reality throughout the tire industry.

In February 1998, Goodyear Tire & Rubber rolled out *Impact,* not a tire, but an ambitious automation strategy aimed at slashing production time by 70 percent and trimming costs by using 15 percent less material and 35 percent less labor. The new process will be introduced to its 85 operations worldwide without the necessity of replacing current plants. The move pushes Goodyear to the forefront of tire automation efforts. The cost-cutting strategies of expanded automation, along with the introduction of technologically advanced products (such as Goodyear's extended-life tire, the Aqua Steel), will push tire prices in this mature industry closer and closer to zero.

Faster.   There is a joke among those who've observed Gillette's devotion to churning out innovative new products: "One day soon the Gillette Co. will announce the development of a razor that, thanks to a computer microchip, can actually travel ahead in time and shave beard hairs that don't yet exist." That's fast! But, there is a hint of truth in the joke. In today's competitive environment, companies are increasingly expected to anticipate and react to future customer needs with products that solve everyday problems faster and faster, that is, provide instant gratification. Kodak's new DC210 camera, for example, allows users almost instant review of their photos. The system converts the image into a document that can be displayed on a television or computer screen. And the whole thing runs on regular AA batteries.

Smaller. Consumers are also demanding that many products be ever smaller. The original satellite TV dish, perched atop a house or dominating a yard, is today the subject of a parody in a TV commercial for DirecTV: Customers are encouraged to use it as an enormous serving dish for Mexican food. The commercial humorously draws our attention to what is happening daily. Everything is decreasing in size, thanks to microchips and other miniaturization technologies. Those tiny, nifty gadgets used by cartoon superheroes and James Bond-types are increasingly available to everyone. The first large, heavy cell phones, for example, have given way to the convenience of extremely small, light phones that fit easily into a shirt pocket. In sharp contrast to bygone days when big was "in," today's consumer believes *the smaller, the better.* Companies are responding with smaller and smaller products like hand-held computers the size of two stacked credit cards and big-screen TVs only a few inches thick.

More elegant. As if smarter, better, faster, cheaper, and smaller weren't enough, the twenty-first century customer also demands an increasingly *elegant* product or service. No more "kluggy" approaches. For consumers, elegance means two things, design and the simple way a product or service solves a problem. World-class design is essential in creating a more appealing or user-friendly product. Understanding the growing importance of design, *Business Week* annually recognizes the best design in products from around the world. And while we tend to think in terms of high-tech, the solution to consumer problems can often be made more elegant through simple means. Grocer H.G. Hill Company addressed both customer environmental concerns (i.e., nonrecyclable plastic bags) and the weight of groceries in traditional brown paper grocery bags by simply adding handles to the paper bags, a simple but elegant solution to a long-term consumer problem. But it's not just retail consumers that want increasingly elegant products. Knowledge Engineering, an innovative Singapore-based computer company, found this out when its customers, highly trained engineers working on artificial intelligence software for factory automation, forced the company to make more elegant-looking computers.

Making everything smarter, better, cheaper, faster, smaller, and more elegant is providing a lifetime of challenges for today's marketer. Meanwhile, customers are enjoying the convenience of finding the best products and services from anywhere in the world, without leaving home, as they shop in a *global electronic mall*.

SHOP IN A GLOBAL ELECTRONIC MALL

Innovations in shopping are nothing new. The advent of the department store at the turn of the century addressed the needs of a new urban consumer culture. Meanwhile, generations of Americans, especially those in remote farming communities, depended upon catalog shopping through Sears & Roebuck (among others) to bring the latest in fashion, housewares, appliances, and even home-building kits. Later in the century, companies such as Avon and the Fuller Brush Company created a dedicated following through the convenience of door-to-door sales.

The small shopping centers of the 1950s and 1960s were replaced by gigantic shopping malls, and traditional department stores by discounters, boutiques, and a whole host of "category killers." By the 1990s, the marriage of communications and computer technology spawned a new era of home shopping that included interactive TV, catalog shopping, and electronic (on-line) shopping. Subscribers and advertisers scurried to partici-pate as growth in these exciting new retail businesses reached into the billions of dollars. The rapid growth of the Internet sug-gests that within the next two decades, retail shopping will shift dramatically to this new medium as it takes over a significant portion of the trade in goods and services.

Television and Internet home-shopping services are expect-ed to grow as new technologies enter the market and provide enhanced convenience and ease of use for customers. Software agents will travel over regular or cellular phone circuits to com-puter databases for electronic shopping, e-mail, and to supply customers with all sorts of information. While some of these things are still in the future, Internet subscribers are already active in cyberspace, shopping in on-line catalogs of major retailers such as JC Penney or L.L. Bean, museum gift shops, and other direct sales outlets. Home shopping—catalog, TV, and Internet—has grown into a $2.2 billion market during the last decade, and it is expected to grow even more dramatically in the future.

SkyMall, the catalog found on most North American air-lines, is preparing for future in-flight shopping via full-color, interactive computers. Using a touch-control screen, passen-gers will be able to place orders for catalog items. It is not too far-fetched to believe that the future may offer on-board, on-line shopping in our automobiles. Mercedes-Benz is already experimenting with multimedia computers attached to car dashboards, and for those in the rear seat, the backs of the headrests. While these on-board screens are intended primari-ly as communication and entertainment systems for travelers, it is possible that they will someday access on-line shopping sites.

Such innovative thinking assures consumers access to a boundaryless world of shopping opportunities, while companies gain inexpensive access to a global customer base. It is estimat-ed that by the year 2000, over 300 million users from around the world will be connected to the Internet, providing a huge potential for the electronic exchange of products, goods, and services. As service providers iron out the question of security on the Net (and they will), consumers are taking quickly to its convenience and lower prices. Big success stories are already evident. CD-Now, a store available only on the Internet, has become one of the nation's largest sellers of CDs, with its huge catalog and extensive information services. On-line bookstore Amazon.com links book lovers to 2.5 million titles. Likewise, Barnes & Noble, Borders, and other major book chains now offer direct sales over the Net to complement their traditional retail offerings. An electronic shopping customer survey conducted by Mastercard International for the National Retail Federation found three key factors contributing to the growth of electronic shopping: (1) increasing dissatisfaction with traditional store shopping (poor service, lack of product knowledge by sales staff, safety); (2) decreasing "technophobia" (fear of computers); and (3) the booming supply of electronic shopping services. In fact, the research found easy price comparisons and abundant product information so appealed to consumers that they were willing to pay more for the speed and convenience offered by electronic shopping.

The Internet isn't the only technology supporting shopping in the global electronic mall. A host of other service providers are scrambling for a piece of the global action. International telecommunications providers are replicating U.S. telephone services worldwide, with global 800 numbers and rapidly declining long-distance costs. In addition, private companies and nontraditional players are also creating new global telecommunications networks that will aid global electronic commerce. As consumers increasingly shop in the global electronic mall, two additional—and challenging—expectations accompany the convenience and performance of these services: Prices and distribution times will approach zero.

DISTRIBUTION TIMES APPROACH ZERO

In the global village, speed has emerged as the new corporate battlefield, as logistics and transportation technologies (described in Chapter 2) drive distribution times toward zero. It's been several years since FedEx changed everybody's idea of distribution with their guarantee of "absolutely, positively overnight, anywhere in the United States." FedEx then upped the ante in the United States by offering *same day* package delivery. And as if that wasn't enough, then they added...*and anywhere in the world in two days.* It is remarkable service for delivery of a small package, but FedEx also makes the same claim for what the shipping industry calls *BUF*—big ugly freight. Until just a few years ago, it often took months—sometimes six or more—to get products shipped around the world. Today the new standard for shipping any product anywhere in the world is just two days.

This new standard for physical delivery has essentially reduced to zero the "float time," at least in the customer's mind, for the delivery of products, services, and information. And it has created an expectation of speed that is challenging every other aspect of business, from new product development to the communication of important company news to employees to providing legal advice. Nowhere has the speed been felt more keenly than in logistics management, where the goals are "time-definite" service, i.e., guaranteed delivery at a certain time on a certain day, and fast resupply of inventories, often within hours. And the increasing globalization of business, in particular the dramatic growth in product trade flows, has rendered all these time-definite goals global as well as domestic.

To meet these stringent new domestic and global logistics goals, many companies have turned to specialized logistics companies, established global joint ventures, and installed shipment tracing and global computer networks to improve distribution services. As with the other aspects of marketing in the global village, however, it's not just physical goods that are facing zero distribution times. The customers for virtually all services now demand faster delivery too. In banking, the number-one dimension underlying relationships between a bank and its commercial customers is speed, faster delivery of corporate banking services. Even in consumer banking, service speed, e.g., teller "wait times," is a major factor in customer satisfaction. And in the brokerage business, the five days it used to take to clear a stock trade, called $T + 5$, has been reduced to $T + 3$ and will probably go to $T + 0$. In almost all industries, the "float time" has all but disappeared as distribution times approach zero.

PRICES APPROACH ZERO

In the past twenty years, surveys that measure the U.S. public's "sentiment" about the economy have shown (with the exception of a few brief periods) remarkably steady increases in consumer confidence, recently as much as 10 percent per year. And why not? Unemployment is at a historic low, and the federal government is now proclaiming budget surpluses (although in reality, the U.S. budget is still in deficit and the government shows no sign of paying down debt). But the real reason for positive consumer sentiment may lie in the steadily improving price of virtually every product and service. In industry after industry, price is at or near the top of consumer purchasing-decision criteria. The increase in the U.S. Consumer Price Index, or CPI, a measure of price inflation for the economy's "core" products and services, has dropped 6 percent in the last ten years, from as high as the teens in the 1970s, to less than 3 percent now. While labor costs are clearly rising, they are increasingly offset by higher productivity, thanks to new "tools" like computers. The other production costs of most goods are declining too, owing to the steadily falling cost of imported components (now a very major part of the cost of cars, for example, and many other products as well) and very modest, if any, increases in the cost of raw materials and energy. Even in areas—and there are very few—where prices are rising, in general they are kept modest by increasing levels of global competition.

In the telecommunications industry, for example, the goal is to provide voice, data, and images in any combination, anywhere, at any time, with convenience, at *very* low cost. To meet the ever-increasing needs of customers for fast, effective, and, in particular, low-cost international communications services,

these telecommunications service providers are creating extensive global partnerships, often between former competitors.
The catalyst in many of these ventures is a lowering of development and infrastructure costs. Savings are passed on to consumers. It now costs pennies for long-distance calls anywhere
in the world.

In today's globally competitive automobile industry, major
producers put unrelenting pressure on suppliers for price
reductions, often automatic annual decreases of 5 percent or
more. In fact, the key player in the GM versus Volkswagen controversy of the mid-1990s was GM's head of purchasing, a con-
summate cost-cutter, who was hired away by Volkswagen to be
the ramrod in their transformation to a lower-cost producer.
Such jockeying of people is a result of the declining consumer
prices of cars in Europe. In fact, one senior GM official refers
to the competition among car companies in Europe as "brutal."
In the automotive industry, as well as others, such reductions
are no longer negotiated; they are simply the new rules of
engagement for suppliers.

Obtaining products and services at the best global price is
an increasingly important goal for the consumer as well. In an
era when consumers have massive amounts of information,
brand loyalty is not guaranteed, and switching costs on the
Internet have been reduced to a keystroke, low price is often *the*
determining factor in a purchasing decision. While certain consumers will also opt for high-price luxury goods, even suppliers
that have traditionally catered to the "status" market are offering lower-priced alternatives. A case in point: Mercedes-Benz
now offers a line of value-priced vehicles called *Smart*.

While prices will never reach zero, the major pricing trend
in most industries is in that direction. Corporate strategies that
recognize the inexorable push toward zero—by slashing design,
manufacturing, and distribution costs and offering "everyday
low pricing"—have emerged as key requirements for marketing
in the global village.

The dramatic social, technical, and political events of the
postwar era—Armstrong landing on the moon, Tienanmen

Square, the collapse of the Berlin Wall—have in some ways masked the equally dramatic, day-to-day changes covered in The Shape of Things Today. We have perhaps become so numb to the constant drumbeat of change that we don't appreciate how far we've really come—as producers, shippers, service providers, and consumers. Those outside business often don't truly appreciate how difficult it has become, with ever-increasing demands for more and better products, faster and faster delivery times, and prices that keep falling as functionality and value increase. But there is even more change ahead, perhaps making this prologue look easy. The next section, The Shape of Things to Come, explores those changes in detail. As you read, keep in mind that the overarching change will be a dramatic one. Everyone—supplier and customer, manager and employee—will cease to be an audience, acted on by events, or in the jargon of the Industrial Age, "a cog in the wheel." Instead, we will become participants, "actors in," or "nodes in the network," as we shape the drama of the twenty-first century.

THE SHAPE OF THINGS TO COME

No one can be totally certain of the shape of things to come, the new world of business. And, obviously, this book presents but one person's perspective on the future—but, it is a perspective forged by some 30 years of business and academic experience, study, travel, and research. The ideas presented herein have also been enhanced through personal interviews with hundreds of business people, in various professional functions, from dozens of countries around the world.

Part 3, The Shape of Things to Come, is not focused on one particular industry or a specific function, like marketing, operations, or human resources. Nor does it take a specific strategic operational focus, e.g., speed, quality, or re-engineering. Rather, it attempts to paint a big picture with a very large brush across the entire corporate landscape, to deal with the big corporate and economic issues in an inclusive and integrated way. As a result, we forfeit some details.

Perhaps as much as anything else, The Shape of Things to Come is about the interplay between the *C*s, *P*s, and *R*s of business. The *C*s of a business are its customers, competitors, and channels. The *P*s are its products, programs, and processes.

Both are clearly changing. However, the *R*s of business, its rules, roles, and religions, are changing even more dramatically. The reference here is not to religion in any formal sense, but to the beliefs systems of organizations, what the people in a company believe about what is truly important in the operation of their organization. And clearly, winning in the new world of business will involve a new business "religion," with a radically reconstructed set of beliefs, new roles, and far fewer rules. The dogma and liturgy of this new religion is being constructed in real time, as executives and employees struggle daily to cope with the chaos in the marketspace created by globalization and technology.

A brief overview of The Shape of Things to Come can be seen in Exhibit P3.1, which contrasts today's world of business with the new world about to emerge. While not exhaustive, this chart provides a brief introduction to the major differences between what we've come to know about business and what we can expect in the future. Much of the new shape of business will defy the old and will present us with what was referred to earlier as "logical inconsistencies," the paradox of two seemingly opposing views held simultaneously. In interviews for this book, managers clearly in tune with the transition to the new world of business were experiencing—or creating—a whole new set of logical inconsistencies. They said, for example:

"We optimize our operations by suboptimizing them."

"We are growing our company by keeping it small."

"We no longer have a formal marketing department; our customers do that for us."

"Our human resource policies are tough and hard by being soft and flexible. We're replacing rules with roles."

The Shape of Things to Come, therefore, may be disquieting to some. And for those who seek certainty and closure, this look to the future may be unfulfilling. Any attempt to "predict" the future is fraught with difficulty. And this book is no different. At the end of the nineteenth century, could anyone have predicted the prod-

The Old World of Business	The New World of Business
Economic Growth Engine	
Information	Bio-materials
Organizational Strategy	
Innovation	Reinvention
Value chains	Value webs
Think global/Act local	Think global/Act global
Perspective, point of view	Pattern recognition
External Focus	
Empowered customers	Engaged customers
Markets/large segments	Customer/segments of one
Market share	Customer share
Market*place*	Market*space*
Channel management	Electronic *keiretsus*
Physical presence	Virtual presence
Marketing	
Internal marketing staff	Customers as marketing staff
Smart products	Continuously adaptive products
Small products	Nano-products
Everyday low price	Prices approach zero
Customization	Personalization
Local price	Global price
National accounts	Global accounts
Global brands	Global icons
Competitive service	Preemptive service
Operations	
Centralized	Decentralized
Sequential	Simultaneity
Fast cycle & distribution times	Cycle & distribution times approach zero
Logical excellence	Electronic *keiretsus*
World-class quality	Customer-defined quality
Fragmented & specialized	Integrated patterns
Internal Focus	
Command & control	Dispersed power sharing
Center controls margins	No center, margins control
Individuals	Teams
Employees	"Owners"/Partners
Rules	Roles
Embedded programs	Embodied programs
Scope/Speed	
Giga (billionth)	Tera (10^{12}); Peta (10^{15})
Micro (millionth)	Nano (10^{-9}); Pico (10^{-12})

EXHIBIT P3.1 The changing shape of business.

ucts and services which have become commonplace at the end of
this century? A recent advertisement from Sony puts it most suc-
cinctly. The ad features a small boy, and the copy reads:

He doesn't know what a phonograph is.
He's never heard of 8-track.
The only time he saw an LP was in his grandparents' attic.
CDs and diskettes are his parents' toys.
What will his be?

Those simple words focus our attention on how difficult it is to
look into the future. The task is made somewhat easier, however, because as we discovered in Parts 1 and 2, the transformational aspects of an era are most visible and keenly felt as we
enter the next. In the Information Age, we witnessed the maturing of an economic era with the development of the global electronic infrastructure, which created a new social and economic
architecture that reshaped whole industries as well as individual
businesses. While one might argue that the global information
network (telecommunications, the Internet, communications
satellites, etc.) is not yet an accomplished fact, it has evolved to
the point that the effects are now pervasive and quite visible.
Industrial Age technologies gave us power over energy, which for
business, created new possibilities for the physical transportation of goods. The full exploitation of these possibilities, however, occurred during the Information Age and were manifested as
a new set of strategic imperatives—meeting the increasing customer demand for better logistical services such as time-definite
deliveries, real-time inventory control, and supplier-managed
retail shelves.

Likewise, as we exit the Information Age, we can see quite
clearly that its major impacts were the creation of the global
marketspace and the transformation of customers and employees into informationally empowered and actively engaged players in the market. In fact, the most important residual impact
of the Information Age is that customers and employees
became the key actors creating the new shape of things to
come, rather than a passive audience being acted upon by
forces outside their control.

Chapter 7 of Part 3 begins by presenting seven strategic imperatives for winning in the new world of business. It then spotlights seven organizations that seem poised to do just that. Finally, it explores seven products and technologies that will be at the center of this new world. While the seven strategic imperatives seem the most likely to create a winning approach to the marketspace, the seven companies are merely representative of the kinds of organizations already taking bold steps to be prepared for the twenty-first century. There are literally hundreds more making equal progress and demonstrating similar inventiveness; space precludes listing them all. And in the case of the products and technologies, those cited appear to be the most promising at this time. However, technologies have a way of surprising us. Some genius in a lab or a garage somewhere may be creating a whole new technology that will revolutionize our world and obsolete this list. In fact, let's hope there is.

- Seven Strategic Imperatives for Winning in the New World
    Reinvent Yourself Daily
    Make Your Customers Your Marketing Department
    Create an Electronic *Keiretsu*
    Personalize Everything
    Think Global/Act Global
    Go Direct
    Replace Rules with Roles
- Seven Twenty-First Century Companies
    W. L. Gore & Associates
    Chaparral Steel
    Granite Rock
    mbanx
    U.S. Military
    Rhône-Poulenc
    BMW
- Seven Twenty-First Century Products and Technologies
    Smart Cards
    Sensors
    Knowbots

Neural Nets/Fuzzy Logic
Smart Materials
Biotechnology
Nano and Pico Machines

To put this new world of business into a broader economic and social context, Chapter 8, The Post-Information Society, describes the shift of power from the center to the margins in nearly every walk of life. It argues further that in the new age, monopolies of all kinds—political, cultural, or economic—will disappear. As such, it concludes, there will be a need to rethink everything. Chapter 9, Every Cell a Factory, contends that while the Agrarian Age conquered hunger, the Industrial Age conquered space, and the Information Age conquered time, the new economic era, the Bio-Materials Age, will conquer matter. In fact, it argues that the Bio-Materials Age is already upon us. Its new technologies are already revolutionizing agriculture (with new types of food and food production processes, etc.), information technologies (scientists are working on a biological computer to overcome the physical limitations of the materials used in today's hard-wired ones), and even manufacturing (with the possibility of revolutionary new commercial materials and "biological production processes").

What happens after bio-materials? It's anybody's guess, but the Epilogue, 2050 A.D., offers one possible scenario.

SEVEN IMPERATIVES FOR WINNING IN THE NEW WORLD OF BUSINESS

The shape of things to come calls for a new set of strategic imperatives, many radically different from the corporate strategies of today. Some of these are just now coming into focus, while others remain illusive. The themes developed in Parts 1 and 2, however, provide some guidance to understanding the new imperatives for winning in the new world of business. For example, the increasing empowerment and engagement of customers will lead ultimately to the customers' role as the prime architects of corporate strategy, intimately involved in all phases of the organization's operations. Specifically, customers will coopt the marketing department's role and function. Likewise, the empowerment of employees will eventually lead progressive organizations to replace rules with roles, as employees define and embody the values of the organization, rather than having them embedded by an isolated management. Management will continue to play a strategic role, but it will be more interactive with the interests of customers and employees. In fact, as suggested in Exhibit 7.1, the traditional pyramid of business may be turned upside down.

Chapter 7 introduces the seven strategic imperatives that appear to be the logical conclusions of today's dominant forces for change. This chapter also introduces seven twenty-first cen-

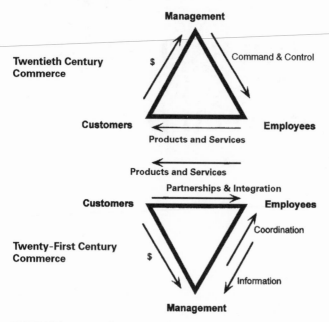

EXHIBIT 7.1 Informationally empowered employees and actively engaged customers create the new shape of things to come.

tury companies that seem to best embody those seven strategic imperatives. It also presents seven new products and technologies that hold the promise of being at the center of the new world of business. However, none of these "groups of seven"— imperatives, companies, or technologies—alone holds the keys to the future. They are simply metaphors for the emerging Shape of Things to Come. Fortunately, some organizations are already providing excellent examples of how to master the seven strategic imperatives outlined in this chapter. Perhaps no company better embodies many of these principles than the much written about and very successful Southwest Airlines.

MAKING SOUTHWEST FLY

In the up-and-down success of the airline industry, Southwest Airlines has shocked competitors with over twenty years of profitability through a strategy of short-haul, low-price flights. Low-cost leadership and exceptional customer value are the corner-stones of Southwest's success. Its low-cost strategy includes: predominately short-haul routes; use of only one type of air-craft, Boeing 737s; no advanced seating; and no in-flight meals. These combined steps allow 25 to 40 percent fewer employees per aircraft and assure low prices for passengers, up to 50 per-cent below industry prices.

Southwest Airlines' culture of outrageousness puts the fun back into flying for both passengers and crew. Its "Southwest Spirit" focuses on being happy in one's work and infuses ground and in-flight services with spontaneity and a sense of humor, while keeping safety and service at the forefront. Southwest devised an organization based on an *inverted* corporate hierarchy, with real power shifted to the employees closest to the customer.

The ultimate customer experience transports a customer from the role of passenger to that of member of the Southwest "community." Southwest listens obsessively to customers and responds to their needs. The airline's success can be measured by its awards for best on-time performance, fewest complaints per customer, and fewest lost bags per passenger. These accom-plishments result from clear company strategies. To achieve best on-time performance, for example, it uses no-advanced seating, no in-flight meals, and smaller, less-congested airports to create a faster on-ground turnaround time.

Southwest Airlines clearly qualifies as the shape of things to come. Embodying many of the seven imperatives described below helps explain how Southwest Airlines and several other successful companies are getting ready to win in the new world of business.

1. REINVENT YOURSELF DAILY

Winning in the new world of business demands daily reinvention. Constant, daily innovation in products, services, organizational structure, production, processes, in fact, in every aspect of busi-ness, is the only strategy that can successfully defend against global competitors, who can easily attain competitive parity in any area of competition—technology, marketing, service, logistics, or finance. Daily reinvention is part of the new shape of things to come because the speed at which global competitors can meet or beat a competitive advantage is now virtually instantaneous. Market and technological knowledge now circulates globally nearly as fast as currency traders move currency.

Historically, elaborate efforts were undertaken by companies to protect their competitive "flanks"; for example, a significant amount of time and resources were spent on filing for patents. In many organizations today, the innovation process is so ingrained, moves so rapidly, and now can be mimicked so easily that patents should be pursued for only the most sophisticated new ideas. The time and resources that would have been spent on patenting new products are better spent on new product, service, and process innovations. As a founder and CEO of a very successful technology start-up says: "We never give much thought to going for patents. Instead, we put all our efforts into constant reinvention of the product line. Let our competitors haunt the halls of the patent office. We'll spend our time creating increasingly better products for our customers at a rate that our competitors can't match."

It's not just small entrepreneurial companies that are embracing constant reinvention. Such well-known giants as Disney, 3M, DuPont, GE, and Rubbermaid are conducting daily experiments with new approaches to virtually everything. Rubbermaid, for example, has as a corporate goal to enter a new product category every year and to always have one-third of revenues come from new products developed over the past five years. Canada's first "direct" bank, mbanx, is meeting its goal of introducing new products at the rate of one every couple of weeks. Such activities are not yet the standard. Only 75 companies are responsible for the 11,000 new products and services introduced from the late 1980s to the mid-1990s. Such companies are instituting new methods to discover and commercialize new products and services, establishing in-house "universities" to constantly train and inspire employees, and experimenting with radically new organizational structures that foster rapid innovation and change.

To ensure that "reinventions" get shared across an organization, a large number of firms, including Coca-Cola and BellSouth, have created the role of chief learning officer or chief knowledge officer (CLO, CKO), many of whom report directly to the CEO. As many organizations have learned, reinvention may be the only sustainable competitive advantage, but unless the learning that goes into it is shared throughout the organization, valuable time and resources are not maximized. Other executives may not carry the title of CLO, but the responsibility is there just the same. While not called a CLO, Anthony Rucci, Chief Administrative Officer of Sears, is playing a major role in its turnaround. According to Sears CEO Arthur Martinez, Rucci is in charge of the Sears' culture of continuous learning, for a workforce of about 300,000, mostly sales clerks and blue-collar workers. Relying primarily on guidance from customer feedback, Martinez, Rucci, and the innovative employees at Sears have driven total return to shareholders to over 30 percent, on average, compounded for five years.

Consultant Tom Peters praises such change agents and calls them "renegades," risk takers willing to take chances on innovative ideas that will improve organizations, products, or services. While product, service, and process innovations are very visible and attract most of the attention, every other aspect of the organization demands constant reinvention as well. One such renegade reinventing the organization daily is Torben Petersen, CEO of Oticon, a global hearing aid company based in Copenhagen. Since taking over in 1990, Petersen has reinvented virtually everything in his organization. In just six years, Oticon returned to its premier spot among global hearing aid companies.

Reinventing Everything at Oticon

Although he is technically the CEO, Torben Petersen hates the title and seldom uses it. A striking individual, tall, slim, with a shaved head, Petersen literally glows with energy when talking about daily reinvention. Since 1990, when he was brought in to ensure that Oticon "never missed another market change," he's reinvented every part of his "knowledge organization" to stay in sync with the rapidly changing global environment.

A global leader in the hearing aid business in the 1970s, Oticon became the largest supplier in the world while product technology and the market was stable. However, Oticon missed the technology and market shift to smaller-size hearing aids, and by the mid-1980s, it had lost its market leadership and was near bankruptcy. A new CEO came in and "stopped the bleeding" by cutting costs and restructuring but was unable to put the company back on track in technology and marketing. Petersen replaced him in 1990.

With 1700 people in 30 countries and $200 million in revenues, Oticon is again the world's leader in technology, customer acceptance, and market share (about 15 percent). To return the company to the number-one position in global market share with the latest and best hearing aid technology, Petersen reinvented virtually everything.

To improve cross-functional organizational performance, he banished the functional organizational structure and created multifunction teams with responsibility for everything from developing a new product to selling it to customers.

To improve communications among "walled in" executives, he moved the company to a new "open concept" building with no offices, even for him, and forced "accidental water cooler meetings" to generate creative sparks for new ideas.

To reduce paper that was "drowning the organization," stifling productivity, and emphasizing bureaucracy over creativity, he threw out filing cabinets and book cases and created interactive, companywide databases with the ability to handle unstructured and undisciplined information.

To keep employees excited, engage their skill sets, and retain those who were valuable but whose skills were outdated, he gave every person two jobs—80 percent of their time in one function and 20 percent in a completely different one—and insisted on constant job-function rotation.

Petersen says he has moved the organization through the entire gamut, from a skill-based to a rule-based to a knowledge-based one. However, he says that it requires "energy, everyday" to constantly reinvent themselves and to keep the organization moving in the right direction. Left alone, he argues, his "unstructured organization" would retreat back to its formal structure and disintegrate.

To keep an organization successful in times of such change, Petersen says, "You need a new attitude and the courage to do something extraordinary." In other words, *reinvent yourself daily.*

Refresh Your Product Line Daily

Innovation has long been most closely associated with new high-tech products, and examples abound. The Nokia 9000 wireless phone is both e-mail and web-surfing capable. Addressing the special concerns of working parents whose children attend day care, IBM and Simplex Knowledge recently developed "I See You" video software that allows parents at work to "look in on" their kids, literally, via the Internet. New digital cameras from several manufacturers use no film, have "windows" that show you the final photograph, and can transfer images direct to computer files or the Internet. And the rage of 1996, the electronic pet, has now "morphed" into an electronic girlfriend!

But all product innovations need not be high-tech. The Cad Flex Arm Desk is built to resemble a drafting table, but it includes gas piston-powered hinges in the legs that allow ease of height change to fit a person's position, whether sitting or standing. Gillette continues to innovate with both men's and women's razors. Even the traditional competitive swim cap received an innovative touch by Speedo, which integrated goggles and cap and reduced water resistance around the eyes. World-class swimmers will use the caps at the 1998 World Championships at Perth, Australia.

Successful product innovators typically spawn scores of copycat products. For that reason, real innovation is not a one-shot deal, but an ongoing commitment to constant, daily, product improvements. Not resting on their "innovation laurels" after inventing self-pay credit card pumps, the major oil companies are reinventing customer "interfaces" to address the need for speed at the gas pump. Shell Oil Company, for example, uses micro-stamp technology housed in a key fob, which can authorize and activate the pump from three feet away and automatically charge the purchase to the customer's designated credit card. Gas purchases become a matter of pulling up to the pump, aiming the key fob, pumping the gas, and driving away. Not to be outflanked, Mobil Oil offers "Speedpass" to small business owners who need better expense records for their traveling salespeople. For a nominal fee, a company can obtain up to ten microchip passes called "transponders" on key chains for the purchase of gasoline.

Many corporate executives don't yet understand the importance of innovation for survival. For companies like 3M, however, innovation is the cornerstone of its goal to meet the changing needs of customers. Beginning in 1904 with the invention of sandpaper, 3M employees have invented some 50,000 indispensable items, including Scotch "Magic Tape™," Thinsulate insulation, and "Post-it Notes™." The company, winner of many awards for innovation, returns over 6 percent of sales revenues to R&D. Moreover, 3M commits itself to generating a third of all sales from products less than four years old.

INNOVATION UP AND DOWN THE VALUE SYSTEM

Another key notion about constant innovation and reinvention is that it cannot be the sole province of one company in a customer value-delivery system. In the future, channel members will increasingly innovate cooperatively to meet the challenges of the new world of business. For example, Silicon Graphics, Hitachi, and NEC teamed up with video game giants Nintendo, SEGA, and Sony to build the next generation of video games. Their combined tactics mirror video game battles in their efforts to outflank, outwit, and outmaneuver opponents in a quest for the flashiest graphics. So fierce is the corporate video game competition that it has been labeled "Sengoku Jidai" after a Japanese seventeenth-century warring era.

NEVER COMMIT THE ORGANIZATION STRUCTURE TO PAPER

Innovation is necessary for products and services, but it is also crucial to processes and structure, in every phase of the operation. Companies wishing to stay on the leading edge must reinvent themselves constantly and find ways to cut costs and speed products to market by simplifying processes and altering organizational structures for greater flexibility. Several companies, such as L.L. Bean, Motorola, and General Electric, have become benchmarks in these important areas.

GE introduced many world-leading processes, such as its Change Acceleration Process, or CAP. At GE, speed, simplicity, and self-confidence are the hallmarks of process innovation in its boundaryless organization. The company utilizes three important but decidedly simple process innovation techniques. *Work-Out* is a method of employee empowerment through which employees from all levels meet in groups to sort out problems and streamline tasks. *Best Practices* expands benchmarking from *what* successful organizations do to *how* they do it in the critical area of process management—moving products through the system, cutting unnecessary steps, and achieving cross-functional teamwork. *Process Mapping* updates the old flow-chart strategy by including customers and suppliers in synchronizing goals and values.

Creating successful process innovations demands several things: an awareness of current strengths and weaknesses (what General Electric CEO Jack Welch calls "awakening"); a clear vision of the future ("envisioning"); the skill to redesign the organization to meet new goals through flexibility; sufficient information flow; and even, when necessary, a redesign of physical space to assure the best use of people and activity.

Companies such as Motorola realize the importance of reinvention by instilling a commitment to qualities like flexibility and responsiveness into its work force. The key to unlocking employee potential lies in continuous education and constant retraining (on average, 40 hours per year per employee) through Motorola University, a benchmark in corporate education. Motorola University was one of the first of what has grown to more than 1000 in-house training and education programs known as corporate universities. But they are more than the old "training department."

GM University, headed by Skip Le Fauve, the GM executive who started Saturn, was established to address certain problems hindering the company: imbalances in employee understanding of corporate strategy; inability to quickly share best practices; and a shortage and poor distribution of talent. But even beyond that, GM University is responsible for ensuring that employees around the world truly understand GM's core values of customer enthusiasm, continuous improvement, integrity, teamwork, and innovation. Established in 1994, following a major corporate restructuring, it appears to be working. In 1997 GM was again the leading revenue generator in the world, and its 1996 profits topped $14 billion, despite continued loss of market share and profit in North America. Although the idea of the corporate university was created in the United States, American companies are not alone in operating such institutions. PDVSA, the $34 billion oil producer in Venezuela, for example, is constantly educating its work force through its International Center for Education and Development, one of only two functional organizations that report to its chairman.

Winning in the new world of business requires constant organizational learning and a commitment to daily reinvention of every aspect of the organization. Nowhere will that reinvention be more important than in marketing, where customers will replace many of the formal marketing programs and professionals.

In the shape of things to come, every person in an organization becomes a marketer, and the old concept of a special group of individuals in a "marketing department" fades into an historic artifact. Successful companies will organize around customers and customer value-delivery processes, not in narrowly focused functional departments. In practical terms this means that new product and service proposals will contain specific and individually identified customers who have participated in the product development and stand ready to purchase the product when available. Businesses will be built one customer at a time, from the bottom up, not the top down.

2. MAKE CUSTOMERS YOUR MARKETING DEPARTMENT

In the new world of business, the best marketing may be no marketing at all, or at least not as it is currently practiced. The central idea of Marketing (the capital M signifying the formal organization, not the functional activity) in the late twentieth century was that a group of individuals within an organization, the *marketing department*, was the customer's proxy, exercising the exclusive responsibility for interpreting customer needs, defining product and service requirements, determining a marketing mix strategy (price, promotion, distribution, etc.), and selling the product to the customer. While great in theory, the reality is that much of it didn't work. For example, some three-quarters of all new products fail in the marketplace.

The new shape of things to come, therefore, requires a new concept that transforms the marketing department and marketing specialists by formally integrating the customer into every part of the organization. With this approach, the customer takes responsibility for product definition, pricing, quality standards, and distribution. The customer interacts with and influences every function in the organization, and focuses corporate effort by declaring, "Here's what I want, when I want it, where I want it, and how much I'll pay for it."

For routine retail transactions, such direct consumer influence may seem all but impossible. But improvements in the retailer's ability to collect, store, and manage large amounts of sales and service information make it feasible for customers, over time, to clearly "define" their needs for even the most mundane goods and services. With higher-priced commercial items, it is easier to see how customer links into an organization can dramatically shape corporate performance.

Customer "Focus" Is Not Enough

Customer focus is the dominant corporate mantra of the 1990s, and with good reason. Every high school student in Junior Achievement and every college student enrolled in an introductory business course knows that everything *should* focus on the customer. However, customer "focus" is not enough; what's required is letting the customer dictate how value is defined and delivered.

Up to now, business has focused on the customer as an audience, for products, services, and marketing communications. In the future, however, the customer will be transformed from *audience* to *actor,* the prime mover in corporate strategy and action. In effect, the customer will dictate what to produce, when and where to produce it, how to advertise and position it, and how much to charge. This new reality is the culmination of the steady empowerment of customers through the last 50 years.

Unfortunately, many businesses, even successful organizations, consistently missed this transformation and consequently lost customer loyalty and market share. The loss of a customer's loyalty can, in many ways, be laid at the feet of marketing, the champions of customer focus in most organizations. Today, many companies that are closest to customers are abandoning some of the traditional and formal organizational aspects of the discipline called marketing. They are getting formal (capital M) Marketing out of the way, replacing it with *customer intimacy,* and assigning responsibilities for customer contact across the organization. These companies are developing new systems for getting customers directly involved in new product development. They are even developing personalized products and services that constantly adapt to unique customer needs over time.

Organizations closest to customers let customers speak for themselves in company forums—from strategic planning retreats to sales meetings to employee forums—to describe their buying criteria directly to decision makers. And those who listen, who make their customers their marketing department, are succeeding beyond their wildest dreams. An excellent example is The Grateful Dead, a band that experienced one of the longest runs in rock and roll history.

Creating Customer Intimacy with The Grateful Dead

Some organizations know their customers intimately and instinctively. Years before most recording artists became cognizant of the need to include customers in their marketing strategies, perennial touring favorite The Grateful Dead broke new ground with its fan base. Using the carefully determined needs of its faithful "Dead

Heads" as a guide, The Dead broke many live concert taboos, allowing a small group of fans known as "tape heads" to stand in special roped areas in order to record concerts. The Grateful Dead was also on the leading edge of technology, maintaining a database packed with tens of thousands of fan names and addresses, which eased the flow of information between The Dead and their fans and provided easier ticketing through phone hotlines. Finally, the death of Jerry Garcia united grieving fans via computer networks, long part of its unique customer relationship.

The Grateful Dead are not alone in getting so intimate with customers that they allowed them to design their products and processes. This strategic imperative requires that companies move beyond the old adage, "focus on your customers," to making customers partners in organizational success. Failure to do so in the new world of business will be disastrous.

Even the best can occasionally take their eye off the ball and fail to get the customer into the planning process early. A reputation for the marketing "golden touch" was not enough when Disney misjudged the food, accommodations, and souvenir needs of its European customers before opening Euro-Disney. The company was forced to make a wide range of emergency adjustments, including closing the 1100-room Newport Bay Club and bowing to European tastes for wine.

And Honda, the Goliath of the auto industry in the 1970s and 1980s, was caught unaware when it failed to adjust to customer desires for minivans and utility vehicles. Honda was forced to back up and reload. The result was its new sport utility vehicle, the Isuzu Rodeo. Similarly, by 1997 Detroit's "Big Three" and Japanese automakers, long focused on popular trucks, utility vehicles, and vans, awakened to the dramatic resurgence of European companies in luxury automobile sales. Flushed with the desire for status symbols reflecting career success, aging baby boomers are abandoning U.S. and Japanese autos for the more prestigious European imports, which now are more cost competitive.

The key to future success means much more than simply listening to customers; it means giving them the power to set corporate goals and design strategy. Many companies rely solely on devices such as customer comment cards as a barometer of consumer needs. But such efforts often only record extremes of satisfaction and dissatisfaction. Addressing customer needs is not just a one-time assessment. It requires constant vigilance, frequent feedback, and updates at all levels of the corporation. For example, the senior executives from all functions of Bell Canada Mobility, a cellular phone company, are required to routinely spend significant amounts of time with customers and then to share their experiences throughout the organization.

Hyatt Hotels, an early innovator in this regard, found a unique way for senior executives to tap directly into the needs of customers as well as employees when company executives initiated "In-Touch Day." This annual program sends managers, office workers, and executives into various departments for first-hand participation in a wide range of hotel tasks, from pastry-making and waiting tables to cleaning rooms and carrying luggage. This personal venture into what customers want and expect is the ultimate in knowing your customers and working them into your marketing strategy. At the Ritz-Carlton Hotel Company, any employee who receives a customer complaint "owns" that complaint. In other words, the first employee to hear a customer complaint is responsible for finding a solution and satisfying the customer. Such policies do not assume there will be a total eradication of mistakes, but they place emphasis on how the company responds when problems do occur.

Chapter 6, Marketing in the Global Village, traced the history of marketing from the mass marketing approach of the 1950s to the engagement marketing of the 1990s (see Exhibit 6.1). An overview of the evolution of marketing and how it will be practiced in the early part of the next century is shown in Exhibit 7.2. *Customer integration marketing* involves not only making the customer your marketing department but also replacing market share with customer share and understanding customer life cycles and the value of a customer relationship over its lifetime—in other words, creating customer equity.

REPLACE MARKET SHARE WITH CUSTOMER SHARE

Making your customers your marketing department places new emphasis on their importance to the company over a lifetime.

	Mass Marketing	Consumer Marketing	Relationship Marketing	Global Marketing	Intimacy Marketing	Customer Integration
Time frame	1950s	1960s	1970s	1980s	1990s	2000s
Focus	Product	Consumer	External environment	Global environment	Customer intimacy	Customer equity
Objective	Profit	Market share	Stakeholder benefits	Global market share	Exceeding customer expectations	Customer share
Action	Sales	Marketing (4 Ps)	Relationship management	Sustainable competitive advantage	Customer engagement	Customer life cycle
Audience	Mass	Segments	Niches	Clusters	Individual	Customer integrated

NOTE: Adapted from Sajev Varki and Roland T. Rust, "Technology and Optimal Segment Size," *Marketing Letters*, 9(2), 1998, pp. 147–167.

EXHIBIT 7.2 Marketing in the global village.

Just as products have a life cycle, customer-company relationships also have a life cycle. All too often, companies place greater emphasis on attracting new customers than on keeping existing ones or even reclaiming dissatisfied customers. But doesn't our own conventional wisdom remind us that it costs five times more to create a new customer than to retain an old one.

Some companies, like Embassy Suites, are proving this daily as they switch their spending on advertising and other expensive media programs (offensive marketing) to programs that track and "reward" individual customer experiences (defensive marketing). The company has found, for instance, that making amends to customers who are dissatisfied reaps big rewards for the company. Customers who complain and get their stay free under the company's money back guarantee of service are several times more likely to return to Embassy Suites than other customers.

Likewise, Chrysler Corporation (prior to the Daimler-Benz merger) exited the market-share game and entered the customer-share business. No longer is it driven by comparing market-share statistics with Ford and GM or foreign competitors. As its mission statement says, it is now focused on "providing the world's highest level of satisfaction with our products and services." That Chrysler recognizes the value of a customer over a lifetime is reflected in its product line, from the first-purchase appeal of the Neon to the last-purchase appeal of the Lincoln and every time in between.

Extending the life cycle of a customer relationship includes first, attracting the customer by offering a superior product or service that meets individual needs; then exceeding the customer's expectations in service, value, and quality; and finally trying to "make it right" when things go wrong and reestablishing communication when customers stray.

3. CREATE AN ELECTRONIC *KEIRETSU*

In the new world of business, when price and quality are essentially table stakes to be in the game, as opposed to points of competitive differentiation, companies will increasingly compete in the area of logistics. In this new world, logistics involves every step of the business equation, from discovering customer needs to manifesting them at the customer's point of requirement.

Logistics, then, is the new basis of competitive advantage, and those organizations with the fastest logistics, who are first to discern customer wants and needs and provide them at the customer's point of requirement, will set the new standard of achievement. Old supplier (upstream) and channel (downstream) relationships with cumbersome formal, manual, paper-based processes will increasingly get in the way. They will steadily give way to new electronic relationships, referred to here as an *electronic keiretsu* (after the Japanese-style "family"-based confederations of companies), in which the "ties that bind" companies together are shared customer focus or shared commitment to innovate around core technologies. For reasons of costs and speed, automakers Ford, Chrysler, and GM, as well as their foreign competitors, have long been linked in sophisticated supply networks based on proprietary electronic (EDI) networks. Now however, others are taking the concept even further by establishing electronic *keiretsus* that can be "hard-wired" proprietary relationships or can use public networks such as the Internet to produce a free-flowing and dynamic interchange with suppliers, channel members, and customers. P&G and Wal-Mart, for example, have created an electronic *keiretsu* wherein P&G directly manages its products (largely electronically) on Wal-Mart's shelves. General Electric, meanwhile, has done away with large parts of its purchasing activities, buying some $4 billion in products and services annually via the Internet.

What is a *keiretsu* and how does it work? In Japan, mutual aid among business groups historically has taken the form of a *keiretsu,* or business "family." Some experts liken this arrangement to a flock of birds whose members fly in supportive formation, sometimes close together, other times spread out, but always in a group. It is this mutual support system that has provided the strength of Japanese business and industry over the past, with stronger members of the group leading, nurturing, and assisting weaker members. As each member gains strength, it has more independence of movement, but with independence comes increased obligation to assist others in the group during times of trouble.

The key strength of the *keiretsu* has always been mutual dependence. And, because it often requires sharing access to each others' computer databases, privacy, security, and trust are prime ingredients for success. The *keiretsu* is a modern adaptation of the traditional *zaibatsu*, the huge, centrally controlled family dynasties that disbanded after WWII. Today's *keiretsu*, however, is still grounded in Japanese culture, which values cohesion over individuality and still rests on subtle management practices that have evolved over time. Because of its unique historic and cultural origins, the Japanese idea of *keiretsu* could not be transferred successfully to the United States. However, the potential for forming electronic *keiretsus* holds real promise for firms wishing to be the first to discover increasingly sophisticated customer needs and "the first market mover" in rapidly coordinating and deploying resources to meet those needs.

A *keiretsu* can be permanent but informal, like the amazing partnership between Coca-Cola and McDonald's. Or, it might be temporary. For example, banks, financial services companies, communications carriers, and computer giants might join forces in various combinations for specific projects and either disband when a project is completed or reform into other groupings. Already, alliances composed of engineers and scientists in organizations across the globe can, as some had predicted, link up over the information highway to manipulate data, real-time shared simulations, and computer design models. These advances in technology are increasingly being employed by electronic *keiretsu* members to combine forces and develop the next generation of products and services. Lehigh University's Iaccoca Institute, for example, unveiled its version of an electronic *keiretsu*, dubbed the Agile Manufacturing Enterprise Forum (AMEF), with participants from over 100 businesses (including members of the *Fortune* 500), universities, and governmental agencies. With members of AMEF, partners use on-line computer hookups to enable the simultaneous performance of tasks, computer control of factory machines, and increased speed for electronic commerce.

Businesses created exclusively for the Internet, such as Amazon.com and CD Now, are particularly adept at creating electronic *keiretsus*, tying together a confederation of customers and suppliers in a sophisticated electronic inbound and outbound value-delivery system. But not all electronic *keiretsus* are partnerships *between* companies. Many companies are awakening to the need for designing interfunctional *keiretsus* *within* their own organizations, aided by the fast-growing technology of Intranets. Some of these are high-tech updates of already existing ideas. 3M's Technical Forum, for example, has been a warehouse of information exchange among the company's scientists and engineers since its formation in 1951.

One of the most sophisticated in-house electronic *keiretsus* is Motorola's global outreach through "scouts" and "trailblazers," who explore business opportunities around the world and establish interorganizational linkages for innovation and shared information and resources. This electronic dialogue, tracked by Motorola University, provides instant information on the company's own business units as well as information on partnerships with companies to obtain innovative technologies or to gain access to new markets.

Several technological innovations are opening exciting possibilities for what's being called electronic commerce on the Internet. Maspar Computer in Sunnyvale, California, focuses its efforts on bringing massive parallel processing into broad commercial use. Through this process, once limited to top engineers and scientists, thousands of microprocessors across company and political boundaries can work simultaneously on different aspects of the same problem. Silicon Graphics, the Mountain View, California, company whose computers allowed movie makers to create the 3-dimensional "dinosaurs" in *Jurassic Park,* is bringing its technology to nonentertainment businesses, allowing them to view graphical data landscapes and apply creative new techniques to imaging specific information categories.

The development of such electronic *keiretsus* will require a reconceptualization of the traditional value chain and value system analytical tools in wide use for strategic company and industry analysis. Such tools create a visual image of the straight-line flow of products and services from static, linear value-creating processes. Many companies and industries—in retail, airlines, computer hardware and software, and even pharmaceuticals—are developing new conceptual frameworks in the form of value webs and value nets. These companies are "clustering" around core technologies or customer values, sharing data, e.g., customer information, and developing joint technologies, products, and delivery systems. The appropriate visual metaphor resembles the hexagons of a "honeycomb," dynamically forming and reforming around changing environmental conditions.

Whatever form the *keiretsu* takes—between or within organizations, public or private, on proprietary networks or open ones—and regardless of the reason its members use it, electronically linking suppliers, producers, channel members, and customers is a key imperative for organizational success in the new world of business.

4. PERSONALIZE EVERYTHING

The ability of today's global competitors to rapidly establish technological parity and quickly mimic perceived customer values—speed, quality, variety, service, and price—is making efforts to personalize everything a strategic imperative. Toward that end, some companies are already implementing some startlingly creative approaches.

In the banking industry, companies are forced into deft maneuvering in order to deal with the seemingly contradictory customer needs of speed (self-service, faster loan approval) and personal, "more-than-just-a-number" attention. Wells Fargo Bank, a pioneer in such innovations as ATMs and 24-hour banking services, believes that technology is the key to balancing self-service with personal service. For example, its computer system expands customer options by providing tellers with instant, personal product and service recommendations based on an individual customer's banking history. Likewise, companies in the highly competitive entertainment industry are finding personalized ways to meet customer demand and build customer loyalty. Blockbuster Entertainment Company is experimenting with computerized systems that will make personal movie recommendations to regular customers based on their rental history.

In the new world of business, the twenty-first century customer will choose from an almost unlimited variety of products and services from producers all over the world. To win customer loyalty, companies must view each and every customer as an individual, regardless of where they are located. In order to understand specific customer needs, companies will use computer systems that allow personal customer data-tracking through everything from point-of-sale to follow-up service information. Meanwhile, though, the increased availability of products from around the world and the rapid expansion of entrepreneurial "niche" players are whittling away at customer loyalty. In response, companies are implementing a variety of marketing tools and strategies focused on addressing individual needs and developing long-term personal relationships with customers. Some such programs are already underway. Among product and service providers, the new "contact sport" is the development of an increasingly personal relationship with customers.

A HIERARCHICAL VIEW OF PRODUCTS AND SERVICES

Too often, products are viewed rather narrowly, often as simply a bundle of physical and functional attributes. However, products (and the same holds true for service products) need to be defined in customer or user terms, that is, the uses to which the customer puts a product or service, even if not the originally intended ones, and the gratification the customer receives from such use. In attempting to determine ways to personalize the product/supplier and customer relationship, it is equally important to view the product or service as broadly as possible. One way to get a broad view is to see it as a "stack" of attributes, from the functional to the symbolic, as shown in Exhibit 7.3. The various layers of the stack can be thought of as follows: the *physical* layer is the design and architecture of parts and material

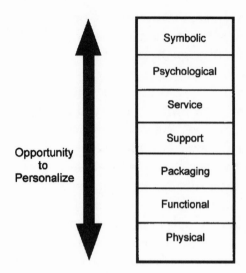

EXHIBIT 7.3   Personalizing the product hierarchy.

(i.e., its shape and size); the *functional* layer is what the product does or how it works, including its quality; the *packaging* layer is, generally, the physical package, but also includes the financing of the product, if required; the *support* layer involves things such as instructions for use and training; the *service* layer includes repair, after-sale assistance (e.g., 1-800 numbers and the like), warranties and guarantees; the *psychological* layer includes the image and prestige that comes with use; and finally, the *symbolic* layer takes in advertising and branding. Each of these layers holds the potential for personalization. In addition, every aspect of communication with the customer offers such potential, particularly as the communication media become more interactive and personal.

INTERACTIVE PERSONAL MEDIA

The growth of interactive, one-to-one media is a critical component in personalization strategies, since building relationships with individual customers requires a collaboration built on data, dialogue, and continuous feedback. In contrast to segmentation, even to segments of one, personalization aims at developing relationships that evolve over time in response to customers' changing life needs and giving customers control over particular products and services.

Retailers of books, hobby products, sporting equipment, and other such products, for example, are using on-line services and reader interest and purchasing records to personally update customers on forthcoming products. Service organizations are likewise personalizing their offerings to regular customers.

Powerful ties between consumers and companies are increasingly the result of improved computer technology. Computerized data obtained from store checkout scanners may indicate personal preferences, the level of brand loyalty, and frequency of purchase. Bit by bit, a customer profile emerges, which marketers can use to personalize products and services. For some, this smacks of "big brotherism." For others, it is simply a high-tech throwback to a time when the small-town storekeeper knew everything about his customers.

What can companies learn from all this computerized information? Sudden switches to low-cal, low-fat foods may indicate a decision to diet or health problems such as high blood pressure. Magazine purchases may reveal something about the purchaser's family status, age bracket, or interests. By tracking parents' purchases for their children, from diapers for newborns through pull-ups, Disney videos, and school supplies, companies know the approximate ages of children in the family and can target families for coupons, contests, new product announcements, and special sales, or tailor products and services to fit individual needs.

A crucial element in personalizing products and services is the awareness of and response to the growing diversity within the United States and many other countries. In the United States, an ethnic, religious, and cultural diversity once limited to larger cities is now a part of virtually every community. Now, many small communities find it necessary to provide special services and bilingual signage for their growing Hispanic populations. Companies such as Wal-Mart are likewise personalizing service for Hispanics by adding Spanish language instructions to signs and electronic credit card scanners. A seemingly simple step, such efforts are greatly appreciated by members of ethnic communities looking for a personal touch in an environment dominated by others.

The push to personalize everything involves two powerful notions: (1) personalizing customer communication through *narrowcasting* of messages and (2) producing *adaptive* goods and services.

NARROWCASTING: CREATING ADVERTISING FOR SEGMENTS OF ONE

Immediately following WWII, broadcasting a marketing message, i.e., creating product appeal for and getting it to everyone, was the benchmark of marketing success. Marketing communication was targeted at millions of "average" customers. By the 1970s, however, it became obvious that not only America but also the world was changing, demographically, economically, socially, and politically. The majority of women worked outside the home. One-parent families became more common. Nations around the world became more ethnically diverse. Western populations were aging, while third-world countries were becoming younger. "One ad fits all" applied no better than "one size fits all." Hence the need for and introduction of the marketing concept of *narrowcasting*, targeting products and services to meet the needs of specific groups. This narrowcasting strategy is used by investment companies, cruise lines, and many others who focus ads narrowly toward the growing number of baby boomers who are aging and nearing retirement. Advertising to ethnic groups is also on the rise: In 1993 $722 million in ads focused on the Hispanic audiences alone (a 14 percent year-over-year increase). P&G's Folger's coffee, for example, is a major sponsor of a weekday Hispanic television program similar to *Good Morning America*.

But narrowcasting goes beyond targeting ethnic or other special groups to communications directed to a specific customer. This powerful concept, aided by technology, will accelerate the ability of marketers to bypass traditional channels and communicate personally with customers. Pushed to its extreme, it will result in personal ads developed specifically for a single consumer. Direct marketing activities now account for some 23 and 25 percent, respectively, of total annual billings of the world's largest "broadcast-oriented" advertising firms, WPP and Omnicom. The world's third largest such firm, Interpublic, saw its billings for direct activities grow from 3 percent in 1994 to 12 percent in 1997. In the United States, expenditures for direct marketing, an indicator of personalized marketing, eclipsed those of mass media advertising several years ago, and outpaced traditional marketing expenditures in 1996.

With cheap but powerful computer tools, companies began developing vast "data warehouses" of information, which was generated by scanners and other devices that allow producers to accumulate information without requiring customers to answer surveys or fill out forms. An excellent example is Harrah's (hotels and casinos), which currently maintains an active database of some 6 million customers and adds about a million new names a year. It tracks individual hotel customer experience through traditional satisfaction information, and it follows gamblers by using sophisticated electronic "slot clubs" that electronically track the play of slot-machine players. In addition, Harrah's purchases credit card data and uses the combined information to build profiles of the most valuable customer types, for whom they develop personal product offerings for future visits to Harrah's. Dubbed their "Total Gold" program and built at a cost of some $20 million, Harrah's uses these centrally managed databases to create personal relationships with customers and take share away from competitors. Likewise, other service companies are making efforts to personalize their responses to the needs of individual customers. Manhattan East Suite Hotel has begun compiling a detailed database on its guests to personalize the interaction with customers every time they need the hotel's services. The results are showing: Manhattan East has been logging occupancy rates of 85 percent, versus a citywide average of 68 percent.

The growth of interactive, one-to-one media is a key in this type of marketing personalization. Waldenbooks traces readers' personal interests and purchasing records, then provides individualized updates on new titles. Along those same lines, Individual Inc. offers customized news services to corporate customers, informing them of changes and trends and the latest news in their industry. Another firm, Heads Up, provides a unique daily fax service to its corporate customers, with short paragraphs on relevant stories and the option for customers to get back to them for the full text.

But, the ultimate narrowcasting in the new world of business will occur when every message, every ad, and every commercial is personalized to the individual customer. New communications and printing technologies are already demonstrating the first signs of personalized communications: ads on Internet sites that are changed to reflect individual visitor interests, magazines with the reader's name on the cover and in the text. While direct mail marketers have long known the benefits of directly personalized material, many print ads will soon be directed by name to individuals. The fuzzy logic of computers will direct printing presses to print a specific combination of ads in a magazine, chosen to fit the purchasing interests of a specific reader. Soon to follow: TV ads produced exclusively for individual viewers. So powerful is this concept that viewers will actually seek out advertising, and in some cases, *they will even pay to view them.*

ADAPTIVE GOODS AND SERVICES CONQUER CUSTOMER TIME AND SPACE

The final frontier of personalization involves moving past the idea of "mass customization" of products and services to the complete decentralization of responsibility for personalization—to the product itself, at the point of customer presence and at the point of customer requirement. The shape of tomorrow's goods and services will differ not just in form but in degree. They will be not only customizable to the individual consumer but also inherently capable of adapting themselves over time. Known as *adaptive* products, such hard goods and services are uniquely tailored to the customer's current needs (customer space) and contain the inherent intelligence necessary to adapt to changing customer needs over time (customer time).

The development of adaptive products and services comes from the realization that the personal needs of each customer differ from all others and also vary over time. Obviously, this realization is not new. What is new, however, is the recognition by both producers and consumers that technology can cost-effectively deliver goods or services with decentralized "intelligence" capable of "reacting" to changes in customer needs over time. An early example is the personalized electronic newspaper, which uses a knowbot or specialized intelligent software (discussed later in this chapter) to individually configure a set of news stories which is then sent to the computer of an individual customer. Over time, the newspaper content gets constantly reconfigured, based on the reading habits and preferences of the individual. Another example is an Internet knowbot known as Firefly, a suite of software products that constantly learns customers' evolving news and entertainment needs. Another software example can be found in some popular word-processing programs, which are evolving beyond the options that allow users to customize settings to individual specifications to include "active computing" features that learn the user's habits and preferences. For example, the program automatically corrects the words most often misspelled by the user.

The auto industry is one of the leaders in adding adaptive components to their current products. Advanced transmissions and steering mechanisms that adapt to driver and environmental conditions and paints that change color and function with customer desires and environmental conditions are two examples. Ford Motor Company is developing headlight beams that automatically widen or lengthen depending on surrounding light conditions. Mitsubishi Motors has announced that it will begin designing the major functions of its cars to adapt to changing customer needs. Such features as transmission, braking, traction control, dashboards, seats, and mirrors will automatically personalize themselves to the driver's size, reach, driving style, and skills.

Chrysler has already started selling a car that adjusts certain functions to the driving style of its owners. Other hard goods with adaptive capability include fuzzy-logic video camcorders that automatically adjust for a user's unsteady hand, a vacuum cleaner that varies its suction pressure based on the dirt level sensed in a carpet, and a washing machine that chooses its wash cycle based on individual washloads.

The development of new high-tech materials (discussed later in this chapter and more fully in Chapter 9) offers additional potential for adaptive products. These include clothing that shapes and reshapes as customer circumstances dictate, surgical instruments that adjust themselves to physician need and patient condition, and high-performance materials that can function as "sensory organs," adapting to the customer's personal needs and environmental conditions.

Adaptive products and services will be possible because of the continued advances in technological functionality and decreases in cost. But the speed of their deployment depends only partially on technology. A limiting factor may well be the willingness of companies to decentralize customer relationships. In the shape of things to come, however, there will be little option but to do so, as competitors from around the world vie for the new global consumer.

5. THINK GLOBAL/ACT GLOBAL

The global village of the last 50 years has forced some hard choices on producers: where in the world to manufacture products and source inputs (labor, material, people, capital, and ideas) and where and how to market around the globe. The catch phrase of the 1980s, "think global, act local," seemed to capture the dominant idea of reaching a global market with a local touch. In the 1990s, the argument appeared that the reverse is more important: "think local, act global." This latter slogan was an attempt to keep a focus on local markets, while exporting marketing ideas and programs worldwide and producing products in the most advantageous parts of the world. Neither approach is sufficient, however, for success in the new world of business, where everything is global—R&D, production, markets, consumers, products, services, prices, channels, promotion, and most important, customers. The approach for the future is to "think global, act global."

As we approach the end of the Information Age, with trade barriers at historic lows and other barriers falling away permanently in the rush to expand trading, every person and every organization in the world is subject to global forces. This is true even if a customer buys all of his or her products locally, or a firm conducts all its business in its own domestic market. When customers gain access to global markets, every company is competing in the global marketplace.

This is most readily apparent in products and services, where it has always been widely assumed that consumers demonstrate a bias for domestic output. The most recent research and practice shows, however, that country of origin (product and service nationality) is not a critical factor in the twenty-first century consumer's evaluation of products. Instead, world-class design and global service, price, quality, and features have become the key purchase determinants. Factors such as brand identity and global standards of time-definite delivery are emerging as the most influential factors in purchasing decisions. Twenty-first century consumers everywhere in the world have similar high standards for quality, price, and performance. In the future, only politicians pandering to minor elements in a local electorate will profess a desire for national products.

Even retail is globalizing, with more and more of the world's retailers doing big business outside their traditional local markets. The French company Carrefour's entry into China is an example, with stores in Beijing, Shanghai, Shenzen, and Tianjin. In fact, European retailers are among the most aggressive globalizers; six of the top ten global retailers are European. Carrefour derives nearly 40 percent of its revenues from outside France.

Charles S. Sanford, Jr., Chairman and CEO of Bankers Trust Company, believes that global electronic bulletin boards on the Internet will be the principal medium through which buyers and sellers describe their needs and execute transactions in the future. Retail financial outlets will be unnecessary because everyone will have global, direct access to financial suppliers through global interactive TV and personal digital assistants. In effect, every household will be a branch bank.

In the new world of business everything must be created and executed in the context of a global market, R&D, production, human resources, marketing communications activities, and all other functions, such as products, programs, TV commercials, and sales force efforts. If they are not already, organizations must put into place plans to make them so.

CREATING NEW PRODUCTS WITH A GLOBAL ARCHITECTURE

Think Global, Act Global is of particular importance when creating new products and services. From the outset, everything must be conceived from the point of view of global consumers in a worldwide market. The architecture of a product—name, functionality, benefits, configuration, instructions, warranty, etc.—must be global. Ultimately, the breadth of a product's or service's architecture will determine its global reach. This means designing to accommodate local differences, producing at world-scale prices and to global quality and delivery standards, and positioning, marketing, and selling to customers across the globe. Auto manufacturers such as Chrysler have already recognized this imperative and now design many aspects of new cars, a bumper for instance, to accommodate all the various standards of local markets into one design. It saves them not only precious design and manufacturing dollars but speeds their entry into markets. Most automakers today are either producing or have plans for a "world car."

While products will always have to be "localized" in minor ways to take into account local conditions and regulations, *brands must be global.* Producers, therefore, will need to understand the evolving role of a brand as a global icon.

BRANDS AS GLOBAL ICONS

An icon is like a metaphor; it stands in place of, or represents, something else. Typically, it is a simple visual representation of something much more complex. For example, part of the appeal of the early Macintosh computer lay in the simplicity of its icon-oriented customer interface. The icon, in this case, represented a very large amount of software code that provided access to a complex computer application. The Macintosh icon found great market acceptance because it allowed easy point-and-click movement through a variety of complicated functions. In global markets, a brand functions much like an icon, easing communication by straddling language and cultural barriers. But it can do much more. It can represent a lifstyle, a whole culture, an entire way of life. Already, many products around the world, particularly American ones like Coke, Levis, Marlboro, Nike, and McDonald's, are consumed as much for their lifestyle value as for their functional characteristics and benefits. In every case, local brands and generics are widely available substitutes, but these globally recognized brands have developed worldwide popularity.

In the first half of the twenty-first century, the globalization of world markets will accelerate, erasing the last vestiges of twentieth-century trade barriers. Global communications vehicles will be commonplace. In fact, some, such as SkyTV, are already emerging. The pervasiveness of information technology will swamp even the most ardent fundamentalist trying to keep an isolated populace immune to the world's voice. The technologies of information, telephony, networking, printing, and the like, will advance to the point that every producer in the world will have access to a clear and relatively inexpensive communications channel to every consumer in the world. And the noise will be deafening! In this global "Tower of Babel," brand will gain even more power and importance.

Recognizing this power, companies like Speedo, Nike, and Starbuck's are even creating their stores as "cultural environments" where customers can deepen the brand/icon association. The makers of these brands understand that icons represent *value by association*. Simple visual images such as the Coca-Cola logo, the Wrigley's gum arrow, or the mouse ears of Disney have a powerful impact in the marketplace. Consumers see the icon and immediately associate a whole body of cultural experience, standards of excellence, and quality.

At best, the brand as icon represents a universal standard of excellence. At minimum, it represents universal recognition, visual appeal, and easy recall. The Marlboro Man gallops across billboards in Sao Paulo, Moscow, and Tokyo as casually as he does in Manhattan. Perhaps the most pervasive global example is the Nike "swoosh" symbol, which communicates in one simple stroke and sound an entire lifestyle and attitude to consumers worldwide.

THE CHALLENGE OF GENERICS

The challenge for local brands is global brands, while the challenge to global brands is generics. Increasingly, generic private labels are able to quickly mimic well-known products, at substantial cost savings. That's why such high profile companies as Procter & Gamble, with their everyday low prices, are recognizing that the magic of the global icon must be matched by the power of value in retaining loyal customers and attracting new ones. As global competition increases, "selection variety" within categories will change dramatically. Retail shelf space will tighten and only the number one and two brands and a generic within a given category will likely survive. Everything else will get squeezed off the shelf.

The secrets to global competitiveness and survival in the brand wars is a combination of value (cost to quality ratio), innovation (through constant product line improvement or new product ideas), quality, and service. This combination leads to long-term success, as demonstrated by leading brands from the turn of the century that continue to move well: Wrigley's, Coca-Cola, Campbell's, and Colgate.

However, value-conscious global consumers are showing increased interest in generics. In the United States, consumers have shown increasing readiness to buy store brand foods at the expense of established brands. Much of this brand erosion has been attributed to corporate diversification, which resulted in brand neglect and slowing rates of innovation. In the UK, a generic soft drink with a taste similar to leading brands has gained considerable share.

Many brand leaders, even the likes of Coca-Cola, are learning not to take brand loyalty for granted. The introduction of New Coke created an outcry among consumers who considered the traditional Coke recipe a national symbol. The company hurriedly returned the traditional Coke to store shelves, providing the New Coke as an alternative. Today, Coca-Cola's global marketing campaign builds upon its strong American lifestyle foundation with carefully crafted global ads that are acceptable to any culture.

GLOBAL COMMERCIALS

Other companies are likewise targeting the global market with a single commercial: British Airways seeks international appeal as "the world's favorite airline"; Kellogg's is taking advantage of global media by airing identical ads in 22 countries with only subtle changes for the different markets; and Taster's Choice coffee uses its episodic, romantic series of TV commercials on both sides of the Atlantic. Similarly, Bankers Trust used a global commercial to tout its global banking relationships.

Winning in the new world of business will clearly require attention to building global brands for global customer loyalty. But it also requires every fiber of the firm to Think Global, Act Global.

6. GO DIRECT

One of the starkest realities of the new world of business is that anyone between the consumer and the producer who doesn't add some tangible customer value will get squeezed out of the market. Retail leaders such as Wal-Mart are cutting the channel intermediaries in their supply chain in order to speed inventory to the shelves. Even where physical distribution or local presence is still a market necessity, producers are often communicating directly with consumers. Giants such as IBM, which traditionally sells its consumer products through a vast retail distribution network, initiated *IBM Direct* to provide its many customers with direct 24-hour service via a toll-free 800 number, because customers increasingly want and demand direct access to producers.

Since market share in the next millennium will depend on strategies that allow speed of delivery and communications to consumers, going direct is an obvious strategy.

Going direct offers a one-to-one relationship, which greatly appeals to consumers. Direct mail, representing the low-tech end of the direct marketing scale, allows companies an opportunity to effectively establish relationships with customers and to provide valuable information about their product or service. Although it has been around for a long time, technologies such as laser printing have brought new sophistication to direct marketing packages. Nabisco, for example, targets seniors with direct mailings as part of its promotional launch for NutraJoint™, a dietary supplement that promotes joint flexibility. Consumer products companies, whose products are distributed through traditional retail outlets, are increasingly going direct to consumers with targeted communications. Kellogg, for example, bypasses retailers with a direct seasonal mailing to consumers, and cigarette producers use similar approaches for specific consumer segments.

The direct mail industry has experienced phenomenal growth, reaching $78.4 billion in 1996. Americans spent an average of $550 each on mail order in 1997, with 83 percent of consumer mail order sales going to specialty vendors like L.L. Bean, Victoria's Secret, and Land's End. American mail order companies occupied eight of ten top spots in worldwide sales. German companies Otto Versand and Quelle claimed the other two spots. While the bulk of U.S. mail-order business remains in the domestic market, improvements in distribution and cross-border customs regulations are fueling interest in global direct marketing.

Direct marketing should not be thought of as "junk mail." Sophisticated multidimensional mailings are now the order of the day. Forrest City Ratner, a large New York City real estate company, used a traditional ad in a daily paper to alert Manhattan-based companies about a new, lower-cost property in Brooklyn—and received no responses. It decided therefore, to use a three-dimensional mailing, sent direct to CEOs. They mailed their 75 top prospects a large, elegant wooden box with a scale model of the building and the neighborhood, each one customized with the respective company logo on the building. Other corporate officers involved in real estate decision making received miniature street signs with a suggestion to take the sign to the CEO's office for placement on the model. Collateral material went to city officials and to rental agents. Needless to say, the building leased in record time.

While some companies are just discovering direct marketing, others have used it exclusively from the start. With excellent products and a dynamic sales force, Dell Computer chose to ignore traditional retail channels and deal directly with consumers via phone, catalog sales, and the Internet. At one point, industry critics thought the strategy foolhardy and doomed to failure. Persistence proved correct, however, as Dell's U.S. unit sales grew a whopping 71 percent in 1996 alone. Dell outmaneuvered the competition by recognizing and adapting to changes in the way consumers shop.

One of the newest and best ways to go direct is the Internet. Indeed, the Internet will clearly establish itself as *the* leader for direct sales, and perhaps for all sales in the twenty-first century. The speed with which Internet and electronic commerce are expanding and the success stories of early participants Amazon.com (the world's biggest bookstore), N2K and CDNow (the kings of direct mail music distribution), and ArtSource (the leading supplier for framed decorative and fine art) are encouraging companies to consider the Internet the best and most cost-effective channel for direct marketing in the future.

Other innovative companies are creating ways to combine the best of the new technologies with the best of the traditional ones. Promoting itself as a universal merchant, Virtual Emporium unites the physical space of an actual storefront with computerized shopping in an electronic mall. Shoppers visiting one of Virtual Emporium's two stores (Santa Monica, California and New York City) can use the store's computers to take virtual shopping trips to any number of retail sites and independent producers for making on-line purchases. This virtual experience offers the thrill of electronic shopping while providing the social interaction of traditional retail.

RESTRUCTURING RETAIL

Analysts in retail often talk about "the wheel of retail," trying to capture the idea that retail is always churning out new concepts but moves in a circle, returning to original concepts every few years. That has never been more true than today. However, the wheel has taken more than a century to turn. In many ways, as we leave the twentieth century, we're returning to the shopping concepts that dominated retail as we entered the century. The Internet, if nothing else, functions much like a general store, albeit electronically, and the traveling salesman who brought goods directly to the consumer's door with a horse and wagon, is back in the form of the Internet catalog and the TV home-shopping network. Retail is being restructured, and the wheel has come full circle.

The centralizing forces of the Industrial Age—high-volume manufacturing, urbanization, improved personal and public transportation, and systems for the mass distribution of manufactured goods—created the centralized, hierarchical corporations and the skyscrapers that housed them. Those same centralizing forces created the multilevel department store and the mass retail colossus of downtown city centers. But the centralization of retail began to break down with the decentralizing forces of the Information Age, and just like the vertical skyscraper and the hierarchical organization, retail stores went horizontal and fled to the pastures of suburbia.

In the 1990s, the first tenuous steps into interactive media and electronic-based shopping led some experts to predict the death of retail as we know it and the beginning of a technology-based shopping culture. Such predictions generate a host of questions and concerns: Will physical shopping space give way to cyberspace? Will malls be diminished to the status of ghost towns? Will the social aspects of shopping give way to the network experience of technology-based commerce?

The changes in retail in the twenty-first century may indeed be dramatic, but perhaps not as one-dimensional as some have predicted. The bottom line is that there will always be a place to shop. Aggressive and innovative retailers are already responding to changing customer and technological dynamics. There is, for example, the recognition that "the mall" is, even now, a "destination" and that shopping is only a part of an overall experience that includes dining, social interaction, and entertainment. We are now seeing the creation of supermalls and superstores that cater to the overall customer experience, meeting needs beyond the mere purchasing of goods and services.

ENTERTAILING

In a move toward what is variously called "experiential retail," "entertailing," or "shoppertainment," malls now incorporate entertainment features such as skating rinks and roller coasters to lure shoppers. Likewise, superstores and small retailers are tapping entertainment as a winning formula for attracting and keeping customers.

Retailers of athletic clothing and equipment were at the forefront of these strategies. Bass superstores provide top-of-the-line equipment for the outdoor enthusiast, whetting the appetite for such adventures with an in-store nature look that includes fish-laden streams, boating facilities, waterfalls, and minitrails. Golf Galaxy includes such amenities as putting greens and on-site golf instruction. And Just For Feet offers fun for all ages (in addition to athletic shoes) with giant video screens, indoor tracks and basketball courts, snack bars, famous-name guest athletes, and even laser light shows.

Not all entertailing is sports-focused. Consumers are also being treated to "eater-tainment" by popular theme restaurants such as The Hard Rock Cafe, Planet Hollywood, and The Nascar Cafe. Normally sedate bookstores such as Book Passages offer customers a wide range of special events, including classes and book discussion groups, while Borders and Barnes & Noble offer coffee, food, and a place to lounge, just like home. And MARS, the Music & Recording Superstore, offers music lovers more than the latest CD or a headset for listening to tunes. The brainchild of founder Mark Begelman, MARS attempts to immerse and involve music enthusiasts in a total music experience. There's an on-site recording studio for customer use, a stage for 5-minute performances, live performances by recording artists, and big-screen tapings of concerts. This new style retail capitalizes on a mix of customer activities, technology, and interaction between the retailer and the customer through special events, feedback, newsletters, and clubs.

Two strategic trends are now evident in the retail industry: (1) entertainment within the retail setting and (2) cost-control and increased productivity through technology. As just described, the first reflects the attempt to combine entertainment, education, and a creative product offering into an exciting, interactive shopping experience that is increasingly perceived by consumers as added value. The second involves the application of technology to customer service and retention, as well as to logistics and sales growth.

In both retail trends, technology is the driving force. Electronic in-store strategies are changing the way retailers assess customer purchasing and service. A variety of exciting new electronic systems have emerged in recent years, and the next decade should provide even more innovative systems. For example, the chairman of Catalina Marketing Corporation urges retailers to forego demographic analysis and substitute "buyographics," an alternative electronic program that profiles actual, individual customer purchase data, as opposed to traditional census figures or overall sales reports. The program rewards eligible customers at the point of sale with discounts. Another example of electronic in-store shopping incentives are in-store kiosks in which preferred-customer cards can be scanned for store discounts and other special services.

Today's intense, competitive dynamics in retail require fast, accurate, detailed information for better control of costs through customer analysis at the point of sale, improved logistics, and inventory control. Tomorrow's retail will require even more. The combination of technology and service innovation that enabled highly focused retailers such as Toys R Us, Sam's, and Circuit City to experience steady growth in the past will require an even greater and faster flow of innovations if they are to continue to compete effectively with the rising alternative shopping channels.

These retailers realize that many new channels will be able to deliver consistently on the convenience, variety, speed, information, quality, and price demanded by customers. That's why they are innovating constantly to meet these needs and are adding the elements of entertainment, surprise, and fun. Toys R Us, for example, already claims one of every five dollars Americans spend on toys. Much of this success can be attributed to meeting customer expectations (of both parents and kids) and ensuring the convenience of a full line of top-quality, name-brand toys. Even preschoolers know that Toys R Us will always have plenty of the newest toy lines in stock. But as competitors increase their ability to match Toys R Us in inventory, logistics, variety, and price, and as on-line shopping opportunities lure parents with hassle-free, low-cost purchasing, the toys superstore may find that it also must lure consumers—from tykes to grandparents—with entertaining and innovative shopping experiences.

Perhaps hardest hit in the restructuring of retail have been and will continue to be the traditional, full-line retailers, who now compete with a whole host of alternative channels, such as focused "catalog killers," TV shopping networks, shopping clubs, discount outlet malls, and the Internet. In recent years, retail giants like Sears, Kmart, and Federated Department Stores have been forced to make drastic cuts, reexamine every aspect of the business and the customers they serve, and occasionally resort to Chapter 11 bankruptcy and reorganization.

One of the most hard-pressed of the traditional retailers was Sears Roebuck. In 1993 it lopped off its ailing catalog division and cut the number of stores and employees in an effort to reverse a downward spiral as consumers abandoned the store in droves. Emerging leaner and with new determination to recapture its customers, Sears, under the leadership of CEO Arthur Martinez, turned to higher-margin apparel and created a new marketing plan complete with flashy ads ("Come see the softer side of Sears"). Other steps in the new plan include creation of database marketing (which utilizes the database and experience of the old catalogue division), along with TV home shopping and the creation of "dealer stores," small town stores owned and operated by entrepreneurs, but supplied by Sears. And the strategy seems to be working.

TWENTY-FIRST CENTURY RETAIL

Many producers are going direct to consumers through outlet malls and shopping clubs. By 1995, Factory Outlet Malls had a total of over 500 malls in operation. Once the collection point used for manufacturing overruns and "seconds," these malls now offer designer merchandise direct from producers at lower prices and are "meccas" for tourist shoppers.

Such successes are luring companies to create flagship stores as a major part of their competitive strategy. Flagship superstores such as Osh Kosh b'Gosh and Nike provide manufacturers an opportunity to present their *entire* line, an opportunity seldom available in traditional retail stores; displayed as the designers intended, in comparison to infrequent or sometimes amateur displays in traditional retail stores; and without the competing voices and product lines of other manufacturers. Meanwhile, old standbys Harley Davidson and the Walt Disney Company, realizing the nostalgic appeal of their products among aging baby boomers and "kids of all ages," are charging into the retail markets with superstores, and Harley Davidson is restructuring showrooms to provide fashionable biker wear for everyone from kids to senior citizens.

As lethargy among traditional retailers forces abandonment of a once-dominant strategy, new innovative players rush in to grab the market. The demise of Sears in the catalog business seemed to open doors of opportunity for other catalogers—from JC Penney, Land's End, and L.L. Bean to Victoria's Secret and the Disney Company. No-hassle shopping at-home combined with high-quality merchandise, convenient 24-hour service, and speedy delivery makes catalog shopping an attractive, fun alternative for many busy consumers. Improved technologies for ordering, tracking, and delivery, along with the availability of home delivery right up to Christmas day, add to the appeal of catalog shopping. In 1997, some $50 billion worth of goods were purchased through catalogs by consumers, and another $30 billion worth by companies. Such shopping is growing at more than 8 percent annually and is projected to reach $100 billion by 2001 and employ some 500,000 people.

The Electronic General Store

In addition to the shift toward entertainment and other new forms of in-store activity, existing retailers face increasing competition from entirely new channels, many of them direct from the producer: TV shop-at-home, virtual shopping on the Internet, shop-on-the-road (in your car, airplane, etc.), and even new vending devices. At-home shopping on the Internet is a major part of the rapidly emerging electronic commerce marketspace, which is estimated to reach $300 billion by 2000. A key indicator of growth is that advertising spending on the Internet reached $133 million in the first quarter of 1997, and analysts agree that the Internet has already gone beyond the realm of experiment into the mainstream of advertising, enabling companies to target specific audiences as more and more potential customers log on. While figures from some analysts put the number of Internet users at 300 to 500 million by 2000, Nicholas Negroponte of MIT's Media Lab believes the number will be more than double that.

Manufacturers such as Toyota and GM, financial services such as Visa and Charles Schwab, and retailers such as Disney and P&G led the nontechnology company spending for Internet advertisements. And companies such as Bristol-Myers Squibb became true believers in the power of Internet marketing when a 30-day ad for Excedrin (during tax season) elicited names and addresses for 30,000 additional customers.

Even grocers, considered by some as, perhaps, the most traditional in their retail thinking, are contemplating the potential of the Internet to change America's shopping habits. Many food companies are already offering the convenience of on-line ordering, inventory, and distribution to individual shoppers.

In addition to the retail potential of the Internet, coming innovations in computer and chip technologies promise to further the restructuring of the retail industry in the twenty-first century. In fact, rather than fewer "points of presence," various retailers may have considerably more, although not always resembling the traditional retail store. In fact, there will be a huge number of "retail outlets" springing up as part of new or existing venues. Among them:

- *Super ATMs:* Will offer consumers a variety of products and services, with their potential ranging from airline and event tickets to placing orders for out-of-stock items or customized products, all with the convenience of a smart card.

- *Super Vending Machines:* Once limited to the dispensing of cigarettes, candy, and chips, the vending machine may emerge as the new automated retail establishment for many product categories, with the convenience of on-the-spot offerings for a variety of products, including hot, freshly prepared meals, CDs, newspapers, and other items.

- *Airline Seats:* As a shopping tool, what could be better than on-board computer links to retail stores and duty-free shops? On long flights, this innovative concept plays to a "captive" and bored audience, armed with credit cards and potentially open to new and exciting products they can't get at home. Already, suppliers of games, news, and entertainment are selling their wares on domestic and international flights.

The wheel of retail will continue to turn in the next century. Where it chooses to roll is anybody's guess. What is clear is that it will include enormous benefits for producers and consumers alike. Society, too, should benefit. For instance, given that the average retail purchase requires some four car trips, there are very real benefits to the environment as electronic networks substitute for the consumption of energy. Much will depend, however, on the ability of retailers to embrace new technologies and innovations, stay tightly attuned to the increasing demands of the twenty-first century customer, and be prepared to reinvent themselves daily.

7. REPLACE RULES WITH ROLES

Throughout much of the twentieth century management theory and practice was borrowed from the rigid hierarchies of the military. Maintaining control within organizations was accomplished largely through the creation of rules governing every aspect of corporate life. In addition to the military model, much of this thinking derived from the necessarily rigid procedures associated with manufacturing and production, which required strict adherence to sequence and form and encouraged the growth of rigid hierarchical structures of command and control. In other words, as the "white collar" service aspects of manufacturing companies began to grow, the familiar and successful centralized, rule-based manufacturing model of organization was imported from the plant floor to the office.

The resulting pyramid organizational structure depended upon a defined set of rules to function effectively. Embedded into employees programs and internal processes through detailed training and procedural manuals, rules served to insulate those in higher positions while controlling those further down. In these rigid environments, performance appraisals were often little more than measuring the individual against these rules.

Since the Second World War, technology and society have changed faster than management philosophy. Today we are on the cusp of the reckoning. From shop floor to executive suite, organizations are struggling to find ways to grapple with the lightning speed of today's competitive changes, to help their organizations think like fighter pilots. Fighter pilots, in command of the fastest vehicles on earth, must learn to instantly analyze and react to fast-changing combat situations and make split-second, life-and-death decisions with no time to check with HQs! Most business situations don't change that fast, but technology is changing too fast for the old rules to keep up. Tomorrow's organizations simply won't have time to devise and implement competitive rules of engagement to cover all situations.

The spiraling growth and confluence of globalization and technology that transformed the world into a global village also forced drastic changes in individual organizations, structure, and composition. During the 1980s and 1990s, the downsizing of middle management and the flattening of organizational structures slashed thousands of jobs and wiped out multiple layers of management. Flatter, leaner organizations and the necessity of team-based approaches challenged companies to rethink rules on issues of command and control in every aspect of work procedures and processes and created numerous questions: What is the new role of management in a work team environment? Who reports to whom? How is leadership within a team determined? How are conflicts solved? How do team members from various departments blend together in a workable unit? Are teams permanent or created and disbanded for specific projects? How can rules be devised for teams whose makeup includes interdependent business units, members from other companies, or global partners?

Companies expanding their presence around the world, which had established rules that worked well and were understood by domestic managers and employees, found those rules did not always translate well for new foreign workers and global customers. Efforts to "command and control" often appeared overbearing and insensitive to foreign employees and customers. Firms seeking to be successful in the world market therefore felt the pressure on their traditional "rule-based" operational systems. Even trying to impose newer ideas such as teams is difficult in certain markets, Latin America for one, where hierarchical structures are ingrained much deeper in the social culture.

Meanwhile, threats to traditional rules also come from technological advances and the declining costs of communications technology, including faxes, video and teleconferencing, cellular phones, and the general digitization of all information onto CDs, the Internet, and corporate Intranets. Informationally empowered consumers demand greater access to all kinds of corporate activities, and the Internet and other technologies are poised to provide access. In response, companies find themselves pushed to provide more information, to include customers in everything from strategic planning to new product development, and to move decision making closer to the consumer. The old rules don't apply anymore.

For companies in large urban areas, the escalating costs of corporate real estate and commuting hassles encouraged them to rethink the traditional workplace. Technological innovations and the increased pressures for work-family balance, including nontraditional work scheduling, dramatically increases the allure of telecommuting as an alternative to the daily commute. While appealing, such innovations create nightmares for rule-based managements.

In such a chaotic and complex environment, where changes and crises occur so rapidly, how can any organization hope to create a specific set of rules governing employee behavior? Most everyone agrees that flexibility is the key to successful modern organizations and that those companies which maintain the old structures, rigid rules, and inflexible internal processes are doomed to failure. Thus, most innovative organizations are rapidly replacing rules with roles, creating a strong sense of purpose and clear understanding of goals and mission and leaving employees to their own devices, absent rigidity.

W.L. Gore & Associates has been on the cutting edge in the creation of new organizational structures. This unique organization, in many ways the benchmark for the new work environment, was the brainchild of founder Bill Gore some thirty years ago. Perhaps sensing the shape of things to come, Gore ignored traditional organizational structures and with his associates, created a nonmanagement work environment with a lattice-work structure that assures ease of horizontal movement and cross-functional cooperation. As a key corporate value, he established the belief that all "associates" should reach their personal potential as leaders and innovators while contributing to the achievement of the company vision. Manufacturing plants remain small (about 200 people), and associates are encouraged to become "product specialists," initiating product ideas, assembling a team composed of various "cells," and developing leadership through consensus rather than decision making from those with certain job titles.

Other bold innovators include Chaparral Steel, the nation's tenth-largest manufacturer of steel. Chaparral's corporate culture is based on treating employees as "adults," a minimum of rules but high expectations that workers will fulfill their roles in achieving the firm's shared mission. Most traditional rules have been tossed. In the spirit of mutual trust, management eliminated the time clock and allowed workers to establish their own lunch and break times. The company tore down boundaries between departments and encouraged cross-functional training. Freedom to act and to take risks, even on the production line, is encouraged; first-line managers can authorize experimental funds to implement a promising idea. The result: Chaparral annually produces 1100 tons of steel per employee, compared to the industry norm of 350 tons per worker, making it the industry's benchmark.

Clearly understanding their roles in company success, the tiny workforce of Investment Scorecard has been known to go all out to meet a new product deadline. Taking advantage of its "no rules, no titles, we-know-what-we-have-to-do" workplace environment, employees once moved beds into the company and worked around the clock until completion of a project.

Organizations don't need to be new or small to take such bold steps. Even well-established organizations such as General Electric understand that old rule-based structures are becoming dinosaurs in today's high-tech, fast-moving global environment, and that adaptability to new ways is crucial to future success. Led by CEO Jack Welch, GE began to take its measure of the new world of business in the 1980s with the creation of what Welch calls a "boundaryless company," focused on commitment to shared values and the notion of continuous change. Within the cultural boundarylessness lies the notion that an understanding of roles must replace a plethora of company rules and allow individuals greater freedom of movement vertically, horizontally, and functionally.

But hierarchical structure and command and control management were reflected in more than just organizational design; they found expression in building design and spatial considerations, never better expressed than through the skyscraper headquarters with penthouse offices for top management and those highly valued "corner offices," which validated middle management positions and reflected an individual's value to the organization. The further down the chain of command, the more likely an individual was to be located in a cramped office cubicle, separated by shoulder-high dividers. Rules dictated not only the assignment of office space but also everything from use of space to allowance for personal touches such as family photographs.

Companies developing role-based environments recognize that as ideas of work change, structural design must reflect and complement those changes. In these companies, flexible work environments are replacing the rule-based office configurations with the addition of coffee shops, on-premise wellness and day care centers, and in some cases, full-time casual dress.

Among the most futuristic of these efforts is the award-winning new headquarters for Nortel (Northern Telecom) in Brampton, Ontario. Faced with the need for a new headquarters, Nortel took over 400,000 square feet of an unused manufacturing facility and created a cityscape for office workers, complete with commons areas, skylight, main street, piazzas, services (including a bank and travel agent), eateries, and even a Zen garden. Workers reside in neighborhoods and can "move" when a new project demands it. Modular furniture eases spatial changes. More important, workers are not saddled with strict rules but are encouraged to explore new ways to shape the work environment.

Chiat/Day, a California ad company, is among those companies that are staking out a place in the new territory of the virtual office, or as managing partner Jay Chiat prefers to call it, the "resource office." Meeting the special needs of the company's "road warriors" and telecommuters, the resource office allows workers to move into the field in areas where assignments are temporary or where sales and customer relations activities are critically needed. Chiat/Day threw out traditional job titles along with the traditional office and replaced them with role descriptions and mobile workstations. Employees spend most of their time in the field. When they need the use of a workstation, the individual contacts the company "concierge" and arranges for phones, computers, conference room space, etc.

Called "hoteling," this concept of road work with arrangements for periodic office space being secured through a company concierge is revolutionary and highly touted as a way of holding down company real estate and overhead costs, while meeting the unique needs of employees and customers in a fast-paced era. Hoteling can keep spatial considerations to a minimum through the use of mobile, miniworkstations. IBM's midwestern division found that by moving staff into the field, reducing office space, and replacing the desk and the bulky file cabinet with the ThinkPad and the mobile phone/fax, the company saw a bottom-line savings of $12 million.

Innovation in the design and utilization of space is a physical manifestation of the underlying need to replace rules with better definition of individual roles and to stretch the boundaries of individual and corporate performance. Like the old skyscraper and the old hierarchical organization, the old notion of corporate rules as a means of control are giving way to the new role-based work environment.

The seven imperatives for winning in the new world of business, daily reinvention, putting customers in charge of marketing, creating the electronic *keiretsu*, personalizing everything, establishing direct communications and distribution with customers, thinking and acting globally, and replacing rules with roles, hold the keys to shaping what is to come. A number of these imperatives are already being put into practice by a few companies around the world. Next is a brief overview of how seven of these "twenty-first century companies" are winning in the new world of business.

SEVEN TWENTY-FIRST CENTURY COMPANIES

The hallmark of the twenty-first century company will be its ability to expect the unexpected, to be faster, more flexible, and even more responsive than in the 1990s. Many have already converted the lessons of the nineties into the seven imperatives just covered.

It is tempting to cite the strategies of some of the corporate giants and true innovators—Wal-Mart, Disney, 3M, Coca-Cola,

DuPont, GE—in describing the twenty-first century company. After all, many of them created new standards in their industries or have survived the vagaries of an entire century. However, several other companies deserve a closer look because they embody many or most of the strategic imperatives necessary for success in the century to come.

1. W.L. GORE & ASSOCIATES

W.L. Gore & Associates, the makers of Gore-Tex, was founded by Wilbert "Bill" Gore more than thirty years ago on the values of a *nonmanagement* work environment and has remained on the cutting edge of new organizational structure and culture. Gore's experience with management practices that other companies are just now grasping has placed it in a unique position in U.S. industry. In 1998, Gore & Associates garnered national attention by placing seventh on the list of "The 100 Best Companies to Work for in America."

Today, this global organization has over forty plants (including seventeen overseas) and its product divisions include fabric, electronics, medical products, and industrial products. The company's unique organizational structure extends to plant layout. Gore & Associates employs more than 5000 "associates," and although plant size is limited to 200, the company often clusters small plants at one site, creating communities of workers.

Company associates are innovative, constantly reinventing themselves and their products. The company encourages all associates to reach their full potential in a variety of skill sets, including leadership, creativity, and individual contribution to the corporate vision. New associates must have a sponsor, but after initial training, they are shown their desks and left to determine their own role in the organization. At various times in her or his career, every associate is expected to become a "product specialist," initiating ideas, assembling teams composed of skilled "cells," and exhibiting leadership in developing cell consensus.

This unique product development style and the company's "lattice" organizational structure means that all associates are equal. There are no fixed lines of authority. The only official titles are those of president and secretary-treasurer, as required by the laws of incorporation. The success of teams and of the organization as a whole depends upon retaining open lines of communication within the lattice structure, letting objectives be established by those who must make them happen, and achieving a group-imposed discipline within this nonauthoritarian environment.

Associates are encouraged to reinvent themselves daily through innovation and the company's no-boundaries culture. The no-boundaries mentality at Gore & Associates is epitomized in company lore regarding one "rookie" associate who joined the company at age 85 and worked there for five years.

2. CHAPARRAL STEEL

Chaparral Steel is an award-winning, internationally recognized benchmark for quality and productivity within the steel industry. Founded in Midlothian, Texas, in 1975, the company is the tenth-largest steel company in the U.S. Although the plant size is limited to less than 1000 workers, it produces 1100 tons per employee, compared to the industry norm of 350 tons per worker. In 1992, CEO Gordon Forward was named Steelmaker of the Year.

A global company, Chaparral's mission is to be the low-cost/high-quality world leader in steel. Toward that goal, workers developed a patent-pending method for creating quality steel with 8 to 12 passes through the system, versus the industry norm of 50 passes.

The focus is on customers. Chaparral Steel's customer service goal is "to be the easiest steel company in the world to deal with." Everyone at Chaparral, even the production employees, is considered a salesperson and is free to interact with any potential customer. Recently, customer service, speed, and production costs were improved with the implementation of a paperless work environment.

At Chaparral, roles replace rules. Within its horizontal organizational structure, only two levels separate CEO Gordon

Forward from production employees, and there are no boundaries between departments. Information sharing and information flow is critical to a culture like Chaparral's, which is based on principles of classless structure, freedom to act, and education of workers. Employees are treated as "adults," without the traditional rule structure. Freedom and trust extend to eliminating the need to punch a time-clock, and workers are empowered to take risks, even to the point of authorizing experimental funds for emergencies or the implementation of an idea.

Finally, Chaparral is focused on reinventing itself through innovative thinking and actions. Even factory floor employees are encouraged to travel to trade shows, visit other companies for ideas, investigate new technologies, and pursue continuous learning programs. Eighty-five percent of Chaparral employees are involved in cross-functional training each year to encourage innovative thinking and decision-making throughout the company.

3. GRANITE ROCK COMPANY

The 100-year-old Granite Rock Co. of Watsonville, California, quarries granite, sells construction materials, and produces building materials such as concrete and gravel. Quality products and customer service are core values at Granite Rock, a 1993 winner of the prestigious Malcolm Baldrige Award. In 1998, Granite Rock was listed twenty-third among "The 100 Best Companies to Work for in America."

Granite's reputation is based on quality through innovative quarrying and materials-handling techniques. It is not the low price leader; in fact, prices are generally about 6 percent above competitors'. But Granite reinvented a mature industry with its innovative approach.

In order to reconcile product/service quality and slightly higher price, Granite makes customers its marketing department by allowing them to define quality and service. In order to assure customer participation and accuracy of information, the company uses a variety of information-gathering techniques including quick-response cards (for instant reaction to service), annual customer report cards (a benchmarking tool for rating the company against competitors), longer surveys conducted periodically for long-range planning, and customer focus groups to assist in probing for product ideas and services. Response to customer needs includes immediate response to complaints with a detailed product/service discrepancy report (PSD). Granite also shares product and company information with customers through educational seminars.

Speed is a critical ingredient in creating customer value. To address customer requests for day-night pickup and speedy in-out service, Granite created the "Granite Xpress" loading system that works like an ATM. It allows truckers to order via computer, check in with a magnetic card, and load from automated overhead bins. The system meets customer needs for speed, cutting trucker loading time to ten minutes, from the industry average of thirty minutes. Meanwhile, Granite's on-time delivery rate increased to 95 percent.

Granite is also on the cutting edge as a company devoted to replacing rules with roles. The company culture is fixated on gathering, analyzing, and acting upon information, beginning with CEO Bruce W. Woolpert and extending to all workers. Management's role is defined as assuring the flow of information throughout the company. Granite's attention to employee potential is also part of the information-sharing process; each employee develops personal strategies for development, education, special training, and target dates for achieving goals.

4. mbanx

In 1996, F. Anthony Comper, President and CEO of the Bank of Montreal, declared cyberspace as the venue for "the next great battle for the hearts and minds of financial services." In less than nine months, the company created its version of virtual banking, mbanx. Electronic banking had already pushed into customer banking services via ATMs, banking-by-phone, and other services. But unlike traditional branch services, banking in cyberspace depends not on finding the "best corner" but on offering full-service and 24-hour access through channel diversity (ATM, phone, fax, PC, Internet). In its effort to continually expand its reach, mbanx is targeting one million Canadian customers by 2002.

Central to the creation of virtual banking is the Bank of Montreal's focus on improved customer service, including consumer demands for anywhere, anytime banking. The major catalysts were increased consumer demand for instant financial information, the deregulation of the banking industry, the globalization of the marketplace, and the decline of banking loyalty among an increasingly mobile and financially savvy population.

The appeal of virtual banking is its convenience and cost-effectiveness. While the cost of setting up its fully functional banking web site was comparable to setting up a branch, the virtual bank has a current capacity to reach ten million households, a figure expected to reach sixteen million by the year 2000. In addition, the average live-teller-transaction processing cost of nearly $2.00 in Canada is astronomical compared to mbanx's cost of 1¢ per Internet transaction.

Virtual banking also allows a new level of personalized service by providing instant data on customer transactions, preferences, and history, according to mbanx President, Jeffrey Chisholm. Utilizing *data mining,* mbanx can tailor virtually all of its services to fit the individual needs of clients. Customers may also use the Internet to shorten and simplify the application process for loans, lines of credit, mortgages, and other services, for which they may receive instantaneous approval, often within thirty seconds!

By listening to and addressing customer needs, mbanx is effectively using customers as its marketing department. But if customers are to define services such as flat fees and money-back guarantees, there must be a sharing of pertinent information. Technology is the key to this information sharing, and Chisholm insists that the criteria for decisions about information technology empower rather than constrain those who use the technology—employees and customers alike. Success in electronic financial services, therefore, is based on letting customers define everything to their personal preferences. Meeting that imperative requires constant reinvention, including a shift in culture which allows greater employee self-management and the flexibility and authorization to address customer needs.

Finally, mbanx is moving ahead of the competition by taking steps to globalize, expanding into the U.S. market via Harris Bank. Near-term international growth into Mexico is also in the works. Even mbanx's name was devised from the start to be global, usable in almost every language in the world.

5. THE U.S. MILITARY

The inclusion of the U.S. military as a cutting-edge organization may shock many readers who still consider the military as the ultimate in rigid, hierarchical, command-and-control thinking. However, this is not your father's armed service. The military's world has changed dramatically because of the sophistication of high-tech weaponry, the speed of information flow, the downsizing of forces since the close of the cold war, and the need to rapidly secure hot spots around the world, often in unison with UN or allied forces. Such factors are forcing daily reinvention of the U.S. military, in the direction of a flexible learning organization.

Just as with commercial changes, military strategy changed with the technologies of different economic eras. The first great shift in military thinking emerged in the U.S. Civil War, when production-line weaponry and the tactics of Industrial Age warfare replaced the cottage-made weapons of the Agrarian Age. World War I brought speed and energy to the fore, as war expanded to the air and the sea. By the 1990s, Desert Storm brought the introduction of Information Age warfare. Every branch of the armed forces adjusted to the new weaponry and the tactical necessity of these phenomena, producing what Army Chief of Staff General Gordon Sullivan has called the first Information Age army. Today's U.S. Army, the best in the world by everyone's reckoning, works with a $60 billion budget—down $30 billion since 1989—and a troop strength of 500,000, a reduction from 780,000.

Speed and innovation are the foundations of the new realities of warfare. During Desert Storm, Lieutenant General Gus Pagonis achieved success in the crucial area of logistics through a unique centralized command and decentralized execution strategy, resulting in an efficient distribution network composed of 50,000 people, 100,000 vehicles, and open-air warehouses. But today, new thinking must extend beyond logistical considerations. The growth of a mobile fighting strategy, the split-second timing of information and weapons systems, and particularly the growing awareness that on-field adjustments to a commander's plan mark the turning points in battles have forced a dramatic shift in U.S. military training. Labeled *maneuver warfare* and initiated by the U.S. Marines (although originally based on German military ideas), the new emphasis is on speed, surprise, and deception. The old military saying that a battle plan seldom survives contact with the enemy is now proving true within seconds.

In the mid-1980s the Marine Corp was among the first in the United States to grasp that the speed of the high-tech battlefield would no longer allow the time-consuming luxury of sending decisions through a chain of command. Similar to new thinking within corporate structures, decision making throughout the military has been pushed down the line. In the new decentralized environment, today's front-line officers and troops in every military branch are being trained to speed up the traditional OODA Loop (observation, orientation, decision, and action) and to respond quickly to changing circumstances. A handbook on maneuver warfare stresses the importance of the role empowerment of troops, a new emphasis on teamwork, and the flexibility to adapt to sudden change.

Finally, the U.S. military is also experimenting with the concept of an electronic *keiretsu*. A brainchild of U.S. Navy Captain Don Nash, the new emphasis on information sharing through computer technology aims to break down the traditional barriers and information hoarding that separate directorates and departments. The goal of the new secured Internet/Intranet system is to share information and expertise up, down, and across, as well as to speed movement of that information to decision-makers at the point of action. Today, the new system is a benchmark throughout the armed services and has been expanded beyond the Navy's U.S. Atlantic Command (ACOM) to include the U.S. European Command (EUCOM), based in Germany.

6. RHÔNE-POULENC

When it comes to reinventing yourself, few companies have taken on such a complete overhaul as France's Rhône-Poulenc under the leadership of CEO Jean René Fourtou. Since taking the reins in 1986, Fourtou has transformed this national company to a privatized world leader in the highly competitive chemical industry through a combination of decentralization and globalization. In the process, the company has become a benchmark in cross-cultural partnership and teamwork.

Fourtou's globalization goals were launched with what he termed his "American initiative," which involved the purchase of Union Carbide's agricultural chemical operations, Stauffer Chemical's industrial operations, and a merger with Rorer, a drug company. By 1997, the U.S. subsidiary was a $2.4 billion business. Meanwhile, globalization expanded on the European front with the establishment of a partnership with Merck & Company, and plans were laid for ventures into the Asian market.

The integration of these global operations with French management challenged Rhône-Poulenc's leadership, as did the tasks of meeting the needs of the new work force and developing new sources of value for its global customers. Decentralization proved the key. The company focused on strategic efforts in areas such as empowerment, team building, and information sharing. Decentralizing efforts included the creation of five worldwide business groups, called "sectors," with each sector having worldwide strategy responsibility.

Teams in each sector gave special attention to breaking down cultural barriers and understanding key global customer value-creation processes. A new U.S. subsidiary, Rhône-Poulenc, Inc., under CEO Peter Neff, forced changes in management with a strategic change from rules to roles. Neff, a proponent of leadership over management, defined core values and established an environment that empowered employees and pushed decision-making closer to the customer. Envisioning his own role as that of "coach, enabler, facilitator, and motivator," Neff challenged management and employees to avoid one-size-fits-all rules in favor of flexibility of movement based on customer values and corporate objectives. Meanwhile, barriers separating functions were removed as members of different departments worked in teams to streamline processes.

Applying team findings to customer needs, including the necessity for personalized service, the U.S. division implemented new programs and strategies. In customer service, for instance, reaction time in the customer ordering process was simplified to allow a one-call, one-minute routine, as opposed to the traditional method which often took days for completion. Such innovation is given priority and rewarded through bonus programs and annual recognition for employee creativity.

7. BMW

Automobiles built by Bavarian Motors Works (BMW), based in Germany, had become a status symbol in America until the recession of the 1980s and the "invasion" of Japanese-built cars threatened to wreck sales. The introduction of Japanese luxury cars of equal quality and in some cases as much as $15,000 cheaper made the 1980s lean years for European automakers like BMW. BMW's turnaround began in 1989 with the introduction of competitive new product lines. In the 1990s, as a major element in BMW's strategy, the company took its first steps toward globalization of production by expanding manufacturing operations to Spartanburg, South Carolina. Its plan for lower-cost U.S. production involved eliminating much of the inventory cost—often the single largest cost component of a car—by building only custom cars, thereby largely eliminating finished goods inventory; radically shortening production time, thereby minimizing WIP inventory; and working closely with suppliers on JIT programs to reduce parts inventories.

BMW's plan is to become the "custom car builder for the masses." With an emphasis on innovation and personalization, this plan reinvents the traditional automaker's penchant for volume manufacturing by allowing individualized orders wherein buyers select "color, interior fixtures, and optional extras" in combinations that make their vehicle uniquely personal. This made-to-order vehicle demands special attention to speed, flexibility, and agile manufacturing in making the necessary production-line changes. To that end, the company is increasing automation and has a built-in organizational flexibility that allows it to adjust to different market contingencies.

The company's focus on customers through its "built-to-order cars" extends to dealerships and to the after-sales relationship as well. As a part of its "Retail 2000" plan, BMW allows dealers to own a second dealership in the same market area. In addition, every member of the dealership staff is cross-trained in areas such as service, finance, and insurance, so that one person may deal with all of a customer's needs. Because of the increase in auto leasing, BMW is making a greater effort to maintain strong relationships with lessors and encourages them to order custom-made autos.

Finally, BMW focuses on the information empowerment of customers. A major step was to set up a website that allows information flow in both directions, providing the company with more customer data while empowering customers with information about the company and its products. The website also allows users to play with the notion of owning a BMW by designing their dream car and trying out other alternatives. Web users can even enjoy a virtual tour in their chosen car, complete with the exciting sound of acceleration.

SEVEN TWENTY-FIRST CENTURY PRODUCTS AND TECHNOLOGIES

As the year 2000 races toward us, could anyone define the products and technologies that will dominate the century? Definitely not. However, the following seven products and technologies appear to have much to offer the world, at least in the early part of the new millennium. In addition to their individual benefits, there may be a great deal of synergy between them. For example, biotechnology may provide the best answer for maintaining the security of smart cards; nanoengines might power a smart surgical device to a remote part of the body for a delicate medical procedure.

1. SMART CARDS

Multifunctional processor chip cards contain integrated circuits that allow information to be stored and processed on the card itself. This technology offers a wide range of applications as well as the convenience of security features such as read-only memory (ROM) and random access memory (RAM). Over time, a smart card will become a highly sophisticated, multifunctional computer on a personal card. It will not only be your own personal bank but will function as your electronic financial advisor as well.

Smart cards will ultimately become your health card, your social security card, your identification card for the office, driver's license, the key to your house and car, and perhaps even your passport. For those who worry about losing such a document, the card itself might disappear into a chip that could, if desired, be inserted under one's skin.

Although still largely in the consumer-testing phase in over ten countries, estimates are that by the turn of the century, approximately one-quarter of all U.S. homes will be utilizing smart cards, and the overall U.S. market for smart cards will reach $9 billion. Using a microchip rather than a magnetic strip, the smart card can be inserted into a card reader for instant service, whether that service is making a purchase, accessing security clearance to enter a building or restricted area, or updating and storing personal records.

The one-card-does-it-all technology of smart cards offers speed and convenience, allowing consumers to use their cards in special terminals. Eventually, a large variety of other devices will be adapted for activation by a smart card, PCs, interactive television, vending machines, telephones, gas pumps, and everything and everywhere that now uses paper money or coins for transactions. The cards will ultimately replace cash, personal checks, scores of traditional credit cards, and even keys. As with all technologies, there are potential negatives. Privacy and security, for example, are of particular concern. However, such issues are well understood and the products will in all likelihood be designed and developed with such issues in mind.

2. SENSORS

High-performance sensors function as "sensory organs" to interact and mediate between the physical world of customer needs and wants and the world of electronic devices that meet those needs. Now widely found in such products as smart air bags, such sensors are finding their way into new applications such as smart courier boxes, whose "skin" contains sensors that adjust to changing shipping conditions, and "smartfacts" that combine smart materials and intelligent artifacts. For example, in a smart highway, sensors could determine and dynamically reassign lanes to support heavier traffic loads. Such sensors are now being developed from a wide range of sophisticated technologies, including piezo-materials (high-performance carbons and ceramics) and nano (extremely small) machines.

3. KNOWBOTS

"Knowbots" (from the combination of the words "knowledge" and "robots"), or intelligent agents, can be thought of as programs that operate autonomously to accomplish unique tasks without direct human supervision. Such intelligent support systems are designed to meet the needs of professionals in a chaotic environment, where time is limited and the demands of work and life require immediate action. The knowbot combines advances in computers and telecommunications to assist the professional in crucial areas such as planning, workflow, analysis, research, strategy development, minor negotiations, and decision making. Knowbots are already moving into many aspects of life, relieving users of mundane tasks. New hand-held "palmtops" and the like are already helping busy individuals keep track of schedules, expenses, and phone numbers. Simple knowbots will be built into all sorts of devices, such as a TV which will automatically turn itself on to the preferred channel at a certain time, or even "tell" the VCR to tape a program that it "believes" a viewer might find interesting.

Today, knowbots are just beginning to appear; however, in time knowbots will move "up the curve" to serve us in increasingly valuable ways, from merely managing data to providing real knowledge and eventually wisdom! See Exhibit 7.4 for an example.

These intelligent software agents are personal devices that serve the user by searching computer networks to locate, retrieve, organize, and submit findings. Like an outstanding butler or personal assistant, these agents will "learn" the pref-

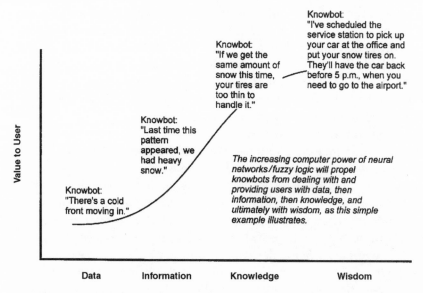

EXHIBIT 7.4 Increasing value of knowbots (example: What to do about the weather?).

erences of their owner and can be used for a variety of tasks. As a research assistant, agents will scan multiple databases and retrieve the necessary information. As a news monitor, the agent may update news items that are crucial to the user on a weekly, daily, or hourly basis. Working as a personal travel agent/concierge, the agent can be programmed to search travel databases for the best airfares, hotel and auto rental rates, and to alert hosts to personal preferences, such as diet requirements. As a personal assistant, the agent can schedule meetings, keep the user abreast of client preferences, and wade through and discard or prioritize e-mail. From a business perspective knowbots will have an even more profound impact, as they become the new "agents" in many markets.

KNOWBOTS: REINTERMEDIATION IN ELECTRONIC MARKETS

Throughout the twentieth century, producers and consumers were separated in the value system by a host of channel intermediaries, including wholesalers, distributors, agents, and retailers. Similar to the turf-protecting strategies of departments within a company's value chain, the tendency was for limited communication, with each channel member pursuing its own goals and establishing its own communication mechanisms.

In the global village all of that was forced to change. Tasks performed by channel intermediaries are increasingly being overtaken by technology, with greater efficiency and cost-savings passed on to the consumer. This resulted in the elimination of many channel members in a process that came to be known as *disintermediation.* In the future this process should continue unabated in physical markets, where anyone between a producer and a consumer who isn't adding value will be eliminated. In electronic markets, however, the *reintermediation* of channels is already under way with new electronic agents called "knowbots."

The word *knowbot* is derived by joining together the words *knowledge* and *robots,* and is a generic term for intelligent software agents that act on behalf of individuals in complex networks such as the Internet. These intelligent agents may take a variety of forms, ranging from software and electronic notepads to robots negotiating neural networks. A consumer example illustrates their purpose. In the past, a real estate agent, insurance agent, or department store's personal shopper would serve as a channel intermediary, finding information, bringing opportunities, or locating specific items on behalf of another person. In the shape of things to come, knowbots will fill these roles. Acting as personal agents, these software agents and high-tech robots will access and manage enormous amounts of information; search for data, negotiate deals, and buy products; and perform many other such tasks, usually within seconds. For example, knowbots will scan daily newspapers and trade journals from around the world and "clip," store, or provide abstracts for items of special interest to the user.

Such intelligent agents not only locate information but are also able to provide job-oriented instruction and advice. Like a personal trainer, knowbots such as "Coach" (developed at IBM's Almaden Research Center) can speed trainees through arduous database training. Coach also provides employees with software agents in three categories: advisory, assistance, and Internet.

These highly sophisticated knowbots will be the user's representative in advanced neural networks, altering the producer/consumer relationship and initiating what Roland Rust of Vanderbilt's Owen Graduate School of Management calls "the age of computer behavior." Serving as an agent, a personal knowbot will interrogate various company computers about the price, quality, and service of a desired product or service and then negotiate the best deal. This new marketing reality will result in companies designing computer systems that are attractive to consumer knowbots and capable of negotiating on behalf of a company. The negotiations between the two will be similar to "my agent calling your agent" to make a deal. The difference is that it will all happen globally, electronically, and at unbelievable speeds.

---

4. NEURAL NETS/FUZZY LOGIC

Neural network technology utilizes "biological" capabilities in both hardware and software to mimic the thinking processes of the human brain. Using an artificial neuron with multiple inputs allows the computer to learn and respond to information and pattern recognition rather than just react to specific commands. The technology lifts the computer's operation to a higher level of abstraction. In 1997, the world received a lesson in the power of this technology when, even in rudimentary form, a computer defeated the world chess champion in a series of matches.

Fuzzy logic works with neural networks and moves beyond the traditional "yes-no" capabilities of computers to handle greater degrees of abstraction and even conflicting commands. An everyday application of fuzzy logic would be smoothing the starting and stopping of subways.

If computers become pervasive enough, an entirely new discipline in marketing might be launched. Roland Rust, professor and marketing futurist at Vanderbilt's Owen School, has suggested that marketers would be wise to begin to look at computer *behavior*. He believes companies will make extensive use of neural networks and fuzzy logic as more and more commercial transactions between customers and suppliers come to be mediated by computers that use such technologies. It means getting smarter about "marketing to computers," he suggests, since they are rapidly becoming important "opinion leaders" in consumer transactions.

5. SMART MATERIALS

Smart materials are so-named because they are engineered with a high level of adaptability to respond to commands and perform mechanical tasks. There are three types of smart materials: *piezo-ceramics*, which expand or contract when voltage is applied directly; *electrostrictives*, which respond to an electrical field; and *magnetostrictives*, which respond to magnetic fields. In practical terms, smart materials are new types of substances that can change their properties at appropriate times to take advantage of a commercial or consumer need. They run the gamut from simple products like clothing fabrics that return to a preprogrammed state after wear to sophisticated medical devices that are one shape for insertion into a patient, change shape while a medical procedure is performed, then return to their original shape for easy removal.

A number of industries will benefit from the development of these materials. NASA's ongoing space exploration means a continuous need for lightweight materials that can adapt instantaneously to changing temperatures and environments. As researchers discover new ways to make materials respond to changes in temperature and pressure, they apply many of their findings to everyday products, such as sporting equipment, household items, and clothing. An MIT researcher foresees such innovations as a frying pan that can signal when its contents are burning.

Japanese research into materials such as fine ceramics has uncovered features that cannot be found in conventional materials—heat resistance, anti-corrosiveness, heat transmission, permeability, and others. These features promise a wide range of potential products in areas such as ecology and energy conservation. The development of a ceramic gas turbine and a ceramic separation membrane that can separate carbon dioxide at high temperatures are just some of the products being actively pursued by the Japanese fine ceramics industry.

Product development efforts by U.S. ceramics researchers are also yielding results, prompting one Penn State University scientist to claim that "ceramics could be the biggest thing since the transistor." Created by using heat and pressure to fuse particles of metal oxides, ceramics can be specially tailored to meet a variety of product needs. Depending upon the raw materials being used, ceramics can improve properties ranging from increased strength to abrasion resistance to heat conductivity.

U.S. researchers are also designing intelligent gels, or "wetware," smart materials capable of altering their shape in response to chemical, temperature, or electrical changes. Others are working with materials that flex like human muscles. The expansion and contraction qualities of these products are especially beneficial for difficult tasks such as driving micromotors, moving delicate items, or adhering to new shapes for medical implants.

6. BIOTECHNOLOGY

Advances in biotechnology over the past decade have astounded scientists and the public alike, impacting everything from pharmaceuticals and agricultural products to environmental products and smart materials. These technologies will be discussed in detail in Chapter 9. For present purposes, however, a couple of the most worthy advances will be highlighted.

The most dramatic advances have occurred with DNA technologies. DNA is the blueprint of life, composed of a chainlike double helix linked together by molecules. Scientific efforts to decode the order of the molecules and their proteins will unlock many of the secrets to life. The Human Genome Project promises to decode the genetic makeup of humans and animals. Future genetic research may yield a new generation of medicines and unlock more clues to fighting disease.

DNA research is also highly interrelated to other technologies; for example, uniting microchip and DNA capabilities to speed verification of specific tissues and lead to revelations about the causes of disease. DNA research is not limited to the medical field. High-tech companies such as Motorola are also conducting DNA research in hopes that gene splicing and genome engineering can have applications for the computer. Smart materials also are increasingly linked to biotech research. These bio-materials may offer solutions to many of the problems associated with traditional materials.

It's important to note here that biotech is not a U.S.-only phenomenon. Of the more than 2500 firms around the world describing themselves as biotech, only 600 or so are based in the United States, although that number appears to be growing. And the number of firms is only one indicator; many U.S. companies engaged in biotechnology are large and have undertaken massive projects. But most in the industry believe and expect biotech to be global in scope. Europe leads at the moment with the largest number of companies, with the United Kingdom, France, Germany, Sweden, and the Netherlands accounting for the lion's share. The European biotech industry, today largely focused on pharmaceuticals, is growing at 100 percent a year.

New companies are also being formed daily in countries like Australia, New Zealand, Japan, and other parts of Asia.

7. NANO AND PICO MACHINES

Nano, meaning one one-thousandth, is now often used to refer to extremely small objects and products. A number of universities and commercial facilities support experimental factories to develop these devices, such as Cornell's Nano Fabrication Center. The pace of development of extremely small devices is picking up, and it's not inconceivable that *nanodevices* might give way to *picodevices,*—one one-millionth, sometime early in the twenty-first century. In developing such extremely small devices, scientists have found a positive relationship between decreases in size and increases in speed, functionality, and value, and also between decreases in size and decreases in costs and energy requirements.

The "micro" era emerged when scientists, starting in the 1950s, figured out how to convert a room full of computers into a smaller and smaller package, resulting in a computer on a chip no larger than a thumbnail. The era of "nano technology" was first heralded in 1986 by Eric Drexler, a researcher at MIT's Artificial Intelligence Laboratory, who declared that although still unfamiliar to most, advances in nanotechnology would propel nanocircuits and nanomachines to the forefront of twenty-first century commerce. Drexler described a "nano" as being built of protein, enzymes, and RNA, and programmed to move molecules into complex structures. In other words, nanomachines are assemblers. They guide molecular structures and are able to bond atoms together in any pattern.

The results of nanotechnology are already starting to affect our lives. Researchers at Northwestern University are sequencing artificial DNA and nanoparticles of gold into structures that may soon provide the "tailoring" of optical, electrical, structural, and mechanical properties for new materials such as biosensors. Meanwhile, researchers in Beijing discovered ways to create ultrathin (4nm diameter) wire called "nanotubes." And

MIT's Gas Turbine Laboratory is working to shrink the PC battery to create the ultimate nanoengine, a shirt-button-size pico-turbine capable of producing ten to twenty times the power of chemical batteries. Nanotechnology will ultimately create a nanocomputer one thousand times faster than today's electronic microcomputers.

THE POST-INFORMATION SOCIETY

Marshall McLuhan coined the term global village in 1964 to describe a world interconnected by a global electronic network. Well before the advent of the Internet, he argued that this interconnected electronic network would function as a "global nervous system," connecting everyone everywhere in the world in a villagelike culture. In a sense, this book is a business sequel to McLuhan's *Understanding Media*.

McLuhan had a rare gift of looking at the world in a way few of us can imagine, and perhaps an even greater gift for describing what he saw in a provocative and stimulating way. He saw the *form* of media (print versus electronic, for example) as more important in shaping our lives than the *content*; hence his often quoted but little understood dictum, "the medium is the message." McLuhan wanted to draw attention to the fact that media have a way of shaping our thinking and perception well beyond the content that they deliver. In the preliterate world, and to some extent the world of many oral cultures even today, since everything was communicated orally, an "acoustic space" was created. A person was literally engulfed by information, much of it coming in via the ear. Because its content comes via the eye, the advent of print created a "visual space" that has long dominated our worldview. In this visual space we perceive most things in a linear, logical, fragmented, and sequential way, just as with the printed word.

Writ large in a society, such linear thinking demands, among other things, specialization for efficiency and centralization for overall system control. McLuhan argued that such a linear mode of thinking provided fertile ground for the development of factories (logical, fragmented production models controlled centrally and supported by specialists charged with optimizing individual stages in the process) and ultimately for nation build-ing—in effect, a factory for centralized social engineering. It is not by accident, then, that the development of the printing press and the culture of literacy in the West preceded the Industrial Revolution and the nation-state. In fact, phonetic lit-eracy was the necessary prerequisite for such developments.

McLuhan believed that the invention of the abstract pho-netic alphabet and its "press agent," the Gutenberg printing press, created a world (again, primarily in the West) dominated by the visual space of literacy. That visual literacy has persisted for five centuries and has shaped our perceptions of all things social, economic, and cultural. Significantly, those raised in this visual space are often unable (or unwilling) to understand the mode of thinking and perceiving characteristic of the largely acoustic space of electronic technologies. With the arrival of electronic media and their growing dominance as a means of communication, however, we as a society have been unceremo-niously "flipped" into this new acoustic space, where the accent is on pattern, the holism, and simultaneity.

What, you might ask, has this got to do with business?

McLuhan argued that the "message" of any medium is the change in scale, pace, and pattern it introduces into human affairs. Business is no exception. Harold Innis, an economic historian (and major influence on McLuhan) persuasively describes in *The Bias of Communication* how individual busi-nesses, entire industries, and even whole societies are shaped by their predominant mode of communication. Daniel Bell's now classic book, *The Post-Industrial Society*, chronicles the end of the industrial era and the transition to the new Information Age. Now, as we move out of the Information Age into the Bio-Materials Age, we are entering what can be called the *Post-Information Society*.

The evolution of the global village during the Information Age created a huge powershift from centralized bureaucracies to small decentralized organizations formerly on the edges of power and influence, essentially a shift from the centers to the margins. This phenomenon can be seen in every part of the country, throughout the world, and in every aspect of life—economic, cultural, social, and political. Once-dominant centers of business power and influence such as New York and Chicago are giving way to a more widely diffused and distributed pattern of power, with, for example, major banks in North Carolina and software developers in Seattle.

Today, many industry observers are calling for American businesses to "prepare for the Information Age," and to implement strategies that will allow their organizations to "effectively compete in the Information Age." However, if an organization is just now adjusting its corporate strategies for the Information Age, it is significantly behind the power curve. We are already in the early stages of a post-information society that will be as different from today's world as the one ushered in by the Information Age.

FROM THE CENTER TO THE MARGINS OF POWER

In the aftermath of the global village, power will rapidly disperse from virtually all power centers to those previously on the margins. The Internet is a prime example. No technology, no political, cultural, or social force is as dramatically global, yet it has no center. It has no center of control, no center of influence or power. Although it could be argued that the United States currently dominates the Internet, growth in hosts connected to the net in the United States is leveling off, whereas international growth in web presence and users is growing dramatically. Although started by the government, it is now funded and managed by its users.

As with the Internet, power in the Post-Information Society, will be more equitably distributed. The global information and transportation network and fast and efficient movement of goods, information, and people that results creates the potential for power to be more evenly and widely distributed. In the future, power will be derived from the global technological infrastructure, not from accidents of history or geography.

Financial power, for example, that was once centralized in cities like New York, Chicago, and Los Angles is now also found in places like Charlotte, North Carolina, home to two the largest banks in the United States. Even the long-established financial clout of Wall Street is suddenly being challenged by San Francisco-based investment banking houses such as Robertson-Stephens, which recently led the nation in initial public offerings. Manufacturing that was once concentrated along the east coast, Great Lakes region, and west coast is now spread throughout the country to areas that offer not only skilled labor and attractive relocation packages but also leading-edge telecommunications services. In the automobile industry, Detroit is losing influence as the most important manufacturing area as power shifts to Tennessee, Alabama, Kentucky, and South Carolina. In entertainment and culture, Nashville and Orlando now compete with New York and Los Angeles, and important arts groups and artists are found all over the country. Even the motion picture industry is dispersing throughout the United States from its original power base in Los Angeles.

Parts 1 and 2 of this book described the disintegration of traditional power structures and cited factors such as globalization and improvements in technology as major influences in the transformation of power. However, this powershift from the center to the margins, enabled by electronics, logistics, and new technologies in manufacturing, is also driven by the absolute necessity to cut costs and be closer to the customer.

With new technologies breaking down barriers, the globalization of the economy has created a worldwide treasure hunt among multinational companies in search of the best new sites for locating facilities closer to their customers. In the global village of the 1980s and 1990s, corporations outgrew their political and geographic boundaries and began to search for people, money, supplies, and customers globally.

A maturing global electronic infrastructure also permits companies to search anywhere in the world for the most cost-effective areas with a higher quality of life than crowded, fast-paced urban centers. High-tech companies, for example, are searching for new locations beyond their intellectual capital in Silicon Valley. Increasingly, the makers of computer memory chips are establishing plants in places like Boise, Idaho, lured there by a combination of lower costs and a better quality of life for their employees. In 1995, none of the ten largest computer chip manufacturing plants on the drawing boards were slated for California.

The southeastern United States has also become a top pick for new corporate site selection—as well as a magnet for foreign investment. The region offers exceptional transportation and a modern telecommunications infrastructure. Cities such as Atlanta, Nashville, Charlotte, and Raleigh-Durham provide a quality of life comparable to any city in the country and proximity to top universities for acquiring talent, providing employee training, and as a source for technological innovations.

Across the nation, small towns and cities are enjoying an economic and employment resurgence. Midlothian, Texas, and Crawfordsville, Indiana, now boast some of the nation's most productive steel mills (Chaparral and Nucor, respectively). Des Moines, Iowa, has established itself as a dominant insurance city; Omaha has become the call center capital of the United States; Seattle, of course, has become the center of all things for software. Attracted by U.S. suppliers and interstate highway systems, foreign companies such as forklift manufacturer Toyota Industrial Equipment (Columbus, Indiana), automaker Nissan (Smyrna, Tennessee), and others relocated their U.S. manufacturing to smaller U.S. cities and towns.

Proof of the geographical powershift in the United States can be seen in the economic rankings of the states. The top ten (based on growth in employment, income, new businesses, building permits, home price, and retail sales) were, in order: Idaho, Montana, Utah, Colorado, South Dakota, North Dakota, New Mexico, Mississippi, Nevada, and Arizona. Five southeastern states and two western states were listed in the next ten rankings (11–20), whereas traditional power states languished at the bottom of the scale: Massachusetts (41), New Jersey (42), Pennsylvania (44), New York (48), and California (50).

Movement of power from the center to the margins extends worldwide. Although New York, London, and Tokyo will continue to hold powerful positions, cities such as Sao Paulo and Shanghai will rival them in prominence by early in the next century. These cities, outside the traditional power structure, will gain power based on their multiethnic composition, outstanding geographic locations, greater access to suppliers and raw materials, and improved worker skill levels. As countries move toward worker skill equity, certain locations will emerge as leaders in specific industries or as high-tech and logistical crossroads. Many of these new leaders will be from countries of the former Eastern bloc, South America, and nations along the Pacific Rim.

The hunger for new markets and the rapid acceleration of regional integration throughout the Pacific Rim nations are creating probably the best global example of center-to-margin powershifts. Once considered the periphery of global business, the nations of the Pacific Rim and Latin America form the new power focus for businesses. These emerging markets have the potential to exceed the combined power of Japan and Europe. Many developing nations are seeing annual economic growth at double-digit rates, and countries such as Vietnam, previously left out of the economic development loop, are emerging as potential key markets for western business.

Even among traditional powers, the new paradigm is apparent. In Canada, the movement from the center to the margins is a major trend, including the relocation of industries and business headquarters from cities like Toronto to outer areas, Nova Scotia, for one. In the United Kingdom, companies are relocating from central London to the suburbs or to Scotland and Wales. As in the United States, these organizational moves are propelled by relocation packages, the promise of lower costs, and the availability of qualified employees.

In geopolitics, decentralization will result in the disintegration of many large national bureaucracies and the creation of perhaps as many as 500 new countries by the middle of the next century. In the United States as well, politicians are now pressing for the decentralization of government in Washington with the drive to transfer many government services, education and welfare, for example, to the states, or in business jargon, to "move the decision-making function closer to the customer."

One particularly important aspect of this center-to-margins powershift is that in the Post-Information Society, there will be no monopolies in technology, economies, business, culture, or politics, of any kind. While the United States will have a military monopoly, it will not be exercisable without global political consent. And while an occasional monopoly might be created by new technology or some unintended regulatory action, it will be short-lived. Information moves too quickly, technology changes too fast, and competitors are too aggressive to leave any idea, market, or profits to a single organization. In addition, governments around the world have largely concluded that the benefits of competition far outweigh those of monopoly.

An excellent case in point is the "shrinking" U.S. monopoly on technology. In mid-century, when the body of scientific knowledge in the world began doubling every ten years, the U.S. share of world scientific output fell from 75 percent to less than 50 percent by the 1990s. This was not due to any slackening in R&D on the part of the United States but rather to the rapid increase in scientific and technical efforts in the rest of the world.

NO TECHNOLOGICAL MONOPOLIES

The rapid development of science and technology in all advanced countries has made it increasingly difficult for the United States to sustain a technological monopoly in many key areas. In 1987 the U.S. share of international patent registrations was 25.16 percent and for the first time dropped to the number-two spot behind the Japanese, who registered 25.88 percent that year. A recent analysis of patent trends among the world's top 200 companies discovered that four Japanese companies—Toshiba, Hitachi, Canon, and Mitsubishi Electronic—topped the list in the number of U.S. patents, with a combined total of 4082. Four U.S. companies—Kodak, IBM, General Motors, and General Electric—followed with a combined total of 3393. Although these margins are slight, the shift indicates an end to U.S. technological monopoly.

Realistically, no single company or country can long dominate any one technology or business. Advancements in technology and the complexity of the markets prohibit any organization from claiming and holding a dominant market position. Increasingly, companies and countries will collaborate around shared core technologies in the type of value webs described in Chapter 7. To keep pace with technological change, some companies are turning to *bibliometrics,* a form of statistical analysis for patents and scientific research, to spot technological trends before they appear in the marketplace. *Business Week* has teamed up with CHI Research to create the global Patent Scoreboard, based on bibliometric techniques.

No Monopolies of Any Kind

The technological diffusion away from the United States will be paralleled by the migration of all other monopolies from their centers of power to the margins. The world's demographic and power structure will be transformed as ethnic groups, visible minorities, and the underfranchised of all kinds gain economic and political equity with traditional centers of power. Several of the more important ones follow:

The Chinese economy will rival that of the United States by 2010.   The World Economic Forum's 1997 *Global Competitiveness Report* showed a surge in China's global ranking; it is doubling its national income every 10 years. The potential of China to go head-to-head with America economically is enhanced by its unrivaled population of employees and consumers, the possibility of its admission to the World Trade Organization, the successful continuation of its most-favored-nation status by the United States, and the addition of Hong Kong's (and eventually, perhaps, Taiwan's) strength to buoy the nation's economy. Of course, much will depend on China's dedication and speed in economic reform and its approach to human rights. However, projections by a RAND study (in 1997 dollars) are that the GDPs of both the United States and China will be nearly identical at $11–$12 trillion by 2015.

The women of the world will gain increasing economic power. Many economic trends and social, political, or cultural issues that develop in the industrialized nations eventually find their way to the rest of the world. The increase in the power of women, economically and socially, is no exception. The role of women in business has changed and is continuing to change for the better throughout the industrialized world, even in such places as Japan, where women had to overcome long-entrenched cultural norms. In many countries, particularly Japan and the United States, women are making their economic presence felt, particularly in entrepreneurial efforts.

Women are now being recognized as *the* global consumers. Certainly this is easy to support with U.S. statistics, in which women represent the nation's strongest consumer group, spending over $2 trillion annually, according to the Direct Marketing Association's January 1997 figures. And according to 1996 projections, the private wealth of all U.S. women is expected to increase to $12.5 trillion by 2010.

While such wealth and purchasing power may not be surprising for western nations, women in developing nations are also rapidly expanding their economic power. Already, the recognition of the business and consumer power of women in less developed countries can be seen in the corporate strategies of global companies. For example, one company's marketing strategy for expanding wireless phone distribution into rural areas of Bangladesh was to allow women in 35,000 villages to take out small loans to purchase handsets and to sell air-time to their neighbors. By December of 1997, that company had some 16,000 subscribers.

The people of the developing nations and particularly the minority groups will be increasingly powerful economically. The democratizing power of information and other technologies are fast empowering people in the less developed countries and ethnic minorities not part of the traditional power structures. That the developing nations are growing today at a rate double, on average, that of their past growth portends even greater economic equity for persons traditionally associated with underdeveloped economies and for those in industrialized countries not of the dominant ethnic population. Thanks to globalization and technological advances, minorities will come to dominate the economy of the twenty-first century.

In the United States, for example, changing demographics reveal a steady decline in the percentage of whites within the population. Currently, African-Americans (30 million), Hispanics (22.4 million), and Asians (7.3 million) are the largest U.S. minorities. By 2010, America's Hispanic population is expected to be the largest minority, at approximately 39 million people, with correspondingly greater political and economic clout. The economic impact of Asian-Americans can already be measured in many of the nation's largest and wealthiest areas. America's Asian population is expected to reach 10.9 million by 2001, with a median household income of $40,600.

Outside the United States, economic growth among minorities is rising at an unprecedented rate, while economic benefits are being more fully enjoyed within national populations around the globe. Global changes in political systems—the decline of traditional one-party structures, the privatization of national industries, etc.—along with the extension of regional trading zones and increases in foreign investment have combined to create dramatic economic transformations for the traditional have-not countries. Potentially big markets are emerging in China, India, South Korea, Brazil, and the seven southeast Asian countries.

Even small nations that were traditionally outside the trade loop—such as Morocco, Botswana, Mauritius, and Costa Rica—are using political reform, privatization, geographical location, investment incentives, memberships in regional trading zones, the creation of their own stock exchanges, and other inducements to lure foreign trade and investment and to raise the purchasing power of their populations.

Faced with the saturation of many traditional markets and recognizing the potential markets in large countries like India (where fewer than 10 million phones serve 900 million people) or small countries like Morocco (where needs may be as simple as water-pumping technologies for 500 rural communities), many corporations are rethinking and adjusting their marketing goals and strategies for the coming century toward greater concentration on peoples formerly in a minority status.

The children of the world will become a major global economic force. Rapid economic growth and a concomitant rise in family income has turned the world's children into a new, increasingly powerful consumer group. Actively sought after by global firms, this new global "niche" is huge and growing, particularly in developing countries. Again, however, the early market signals are easiest to read in the West.

Predictions by the U.S. Census Bureau show that by the year 2006, the number of teenagers in the United States will reach an astonishing 30.8 million, almost one million more than the total for baby boomer teens in the 1960s and 1970s. The purchasing power of these teens is likewise expected to explode. Today, spending for U.S. teens between the ages of 12 and 19 exceeds $108 billion. Major categories for purchases include athletic shoes, general clothing, blue jeans, groceries, and health and beauty aids. As teens gain more access to credit cards, phone cards, and other purchasing power conveniences, their appeal to marketers increases. And when U.S. teen purchasing power is combined with that of teens in other parts of the world (all of whom want basically the same things), it is no surprise that they are considered by some to be "the biggest wave yet."

Increase in global governance. While a few countries have tended to dominate global politics, political power is slowly but surely diffusing from the center to the margins. Despite the formation of smaller and smaller countries better able to govern themselves as decentralized units, the trend toward global governance in certain matters will continue. Increasing reliance on the UN for peacekeeping is one example. Another is the near-universal agreement on land mines signed in late 1997. Others include the evolution of GATT to the World Trade Organization and the growing global governance of the physical environment.

Between 1974 and 1994, for example, some 170 global treaties were created to focus on some aspect of global environmental management, including such notable ones as the Convention on International Trade in Endangered Species; the Montreal Protocol, which regulated the use of CFCs; the London Dumping Convention; and the Rio de Janeiro Accord, signed by 100 countries. By late 1997, countries from around the world, meeting in Kyoto, Japan, as part of a UN effort, seemed to be moving toward accord on issues such as global warming.

Clearly, the regulation of industry and international business is increasingly moving beyond the control of individual nations and into that of a veritable alphabet soup of international agencies and trade alliances, including WTO, the EU, and NAFTA. Among the new batch of free-trade initiatives, the most closely watched include the highly touted "Miami Process," the Asia-Pacific Economic Cooperation (APEC), and ASEAN. Also of keen interest is the potential for cooperation within emerging markets throughout the Middle East, including Egypt, Israel, Palestine, Jordan, and Lebanon.

This is not to say that these trade and economic cooperation pacts will regulate the global political environment. But such pacts are a leading indicator that matters of global concern are indeed receiving global attention. In this connection, it's interesting to recall that the present day European Union started out as a limited agreement on coal production among a few European countries. More global agreements can be expected in the twenty-first century, covering diverse areas of global concern—water use, cross-border data and communications flows, and human and individual rights, to name a few.

RETHINKING EVERYTHING

Many organizations today find they have about the same life expectancy as a major league baseball player's career. They are discovering that being flexible, prepared for constant change, demands rethinking everything.

RETHINKING THE ECONOMICS OF BUSINESS

MIT economist Paul Krugman has been quoted as saying there are three types of economics: the *up-and-down economics* usually associated with the stock market and government economic indicators; *airport bookstore economics*, which warns about such things as impending global depression; and the mathematical, *Greek-letter economics* of the academicians. This latter form arose from the self-perceived need of economists in the 1870s to be more "scientific." They borrowed their approach from successful physicists of the day, who were convincingly converting physical phenomena into Greek-letter formulas. While fine for theoretical economists, the problem is that it formed the roots of management thinking and still dominates it today.

Conventional management thinking, then, depends on a metaphor of economics that is based tenuously on the laws of physical phenomena. As McKinsey consultant Eric Beinhocker argues, such an approach "makes three important assumptions: (1) that the industry structure is known, (2) that the diminishing returns law applies, and (3) that all firms are perfectly rational." In today's world, however, none of these assumptions holds true. For example, firms seldom have identical information, therefore negating rationality, and industry structures are changing dramatically and unpredictably. Perhaps most challenging, however, is that in today's increasingly important marketspaces, like the Internet, the law of diminishing returns (i.e., each new entrant to a market diminishes the returns for all existing firms) does not apply. Thus, in rethinking economics, we are beginning to understand, for example, that every new entrant to the Internet geometrically increases the value of each current participant.

As we enter the Post-Information Society, we are just coming to realize that it is inclusion and participation that expand value and wealth, and that power shared is power gained. Greek-letter economics holds no weight in the mature phase of the Information Age.

RETHINKING CORPORATE STRATEGY

The arrival of the global village, with its ubiquitous and inexpensive information technologies, forced all companies to rethink many of their tactical operating processes. However, some companies, and not just information-based ones, now need to rethink the strategic fundamentals of their businesses. A case in point is the near demise of *Encyclopedia Britannica*, one of the world's best brands, at the hands of Encarta, the CD-ROM version from Microsoft. The Britannica encyclopedia sells for nearly $2000, whereas you can buy the Microsoft version for under $50. Encarta 98, the latest version, includes 32,000 articles, 14,000 photos and illustrations, dozens of sound clips and "virtual tours" with links and sidebars, electronically indexed content, and software tools for assembling research reports with all sources automatically cited. All this is bundled into computer operating software or contained in two CDs weighing a few ounces. It's no contest compared to the unwieldy bulk and corresponding cost (printing, distribution, etc.) of Britannica. Of course, Britannica is now in the market with a computer-based product, but only time will tell if it's too little too late.

This story illustrates the need to rethink the rules of competition, since competitors using information as a strategy can obsolete virtually any traditional source of competitive advantage. Just as all companies became global in the 1990s, in the future, all companies will be information companies. If such a statement seems dubious, think through the economics of virtually any business, even heavy industry. Most of the "value" for which customers pay is represented not by raw materials and manufacturing costs but by "information" in the form of engineering, sales, service, management overhead, and the like.

For corporations, strategic flexibility presupposes real employee empowerment, information sharing, and new ways of redistributing power among partners, suppliers, and customers. Some of today's most successful companies are those whose corporate culture was infused with the idea of flexibility from the outset. For example, W.L. Gore & Associates was built on the ideas of informal structure, teamwork, information sharing, and participation decades before such ideas came into fashion.

Getting flexible and staying flexible is tough, costly, and demanding. Perhaps the most difficult aspect is relinquishing a large share of power to others—customers, partners, and colleagues. But as technology and globalization establish competitive parity in most industries, companies are more dependent than ever on a complex set of corporate alliances.

The early 1998 announcement of an alliance between Continental Airlines and Northwest Airlines is but the latest in a series of what are being called *virtual alliances*. At the heart of this alliance is information—"code sharing" of flight schedules and customer frequent-flier programs. Such semimergers, according to airline industry analysts, offer the advantages of building critical mass while avoiding the logistical and legal complexities of a full merger. They also offer protection against being acquired outright.

No doubt, some deceased CEOs are turning in their graves as many corporate managers today are rethinking strategy, granting veto power to self-directed employee work teams, forming alliances with competitors, and putting customers in charge of many aspects of the corporate organization.

RETHINKING COMPETITION

By necessity, the automobile industry was among the leaders in responding to globalization in the postwar era. Automakers have been competing to be the first to design, build, and market a "world car." Ford's first attempt, the Mondeo, was an international effort pulling together design and engineering expertise from the United States, Germany, and England in an eight-year, multimillion-dollar project.

Automakers had to rethink everything as they moved beyond national boundaries—Mercury in Mexico, Nissan in Tennessee, and BMW in South Carolina, to name a few—and participated in multinational joint ventures between competitors, such as Mitsubishi with Daimler-Benz and Ford with Volkswagen.

In industry after industry, even while rivalry grows in intensity, the "us vs. them" competitive mentality is giving way to partnerships and "cooperation for mutual benefit." For example, in the mid-1990s, twenty major corporations based in

California's famous Silicon Valley joined forces to create an electronic marketplace dubbed CommerceNet. The companies, among them giants Intel, PacBell, Sun Microsystems, and Hewlett Packard, created a virtual marketspace on the Internet. CommerceNet's intent is to move information through Silicon Valley at warp speed, with services including advertising through multimedia catalogs, network access to multiple computers through hypertext, and pricing services through shopping agents. Consumers are allowed remote access to "test drive" components before they hit the markets. Participating corporations benefit as well. Electronic contracting systems speed deals and circulate money through cyberspace. Software enables engineers and research departments from several companies to collaborate in creating new products and services.

Complex products and markets often require several companies to join forces. Working together, virtual corporations large and small are dramatically demonstrating improved speed and flexibility in bringing new services and products to customers. Using electronic information networks, tightly focused and specialized organizations form and re-form instantly to take advantage of surprise opportunities. Each partner contributes its core competency and shares in costs and market access. This allows even small entrepreneurial firms the opportunity to participate in major marketing ventures, while large companies enjoy the benefits of speed without bulk. Uniting their expertise and carefully developing goals and temporary work structures, corporations of all sizes improve their abilities to react to market forces and consumer needs.

The speed and force with which digital technologies change the competitive marketplace rival the impact of Gutenberg's press. Digital technology gives access to a virtual marketplace where anyone can buy anything, link up with anyone, or conduct business anywhere in the world. For example, Microsoft's Nathan Myhrvold, vice president of advanced technology, noted in 1994 that "few cars are sold through the Info Highway. But people will figure out how to do it." Four years later, the Internet had become an active and viable sales channel for both new and used cars. Myhrvold and his boss, Bill Gates, are doing more than just rethinking current competition for their products. They are totally rethinking the computer itself, aided by top global researchers. The overarching goal is to make computers not merely more interactive but more capable of mimicking human intelligence. They want to create PCs that "listen," "speak," "see," and "learn." Dr. Robert Metcalfe, inventor of the Ethernet, a now common networking standard, argues, that Gates and Microsoft may need to rethink again. "PCs," he predicted in 1998, "are passé. Various forms of network computers...will replace the Wintel clunkers we enjoy today. And you won't have to carry your computers so much anymore, as there will be one waiting for you where you're going."

RETHINKING GLOBAL COMPETITIVENESS

In a special issue of *Business Week* in the mid-1990s, entitled "21st Century Capitalism," editors described many of the technology, manufacturing, and financial trends in the new world of business that are causing continued rethinking of stereotypes about regional and national competitiveness. Among them:

- Latin America—although not generally associated with high tech, it is "absorbing high-tech investment faster per capita than the Pacific Rim."

- Southeast Asia—rapidly switching from "low-skill manufacturing" to product design with movement into chip packaging (Malaysia), consumer electronics (Hong Kong), and its first tentative steps in aerospace (Taiwan) and biotechnology (Singapore). South Korea, despite its recent bout with "Asian Flu," is no longer a place for low-cost manufacturing, but sports a rich diversified service economy and actively exports manufacturing jobs to low-wage Southeast Asian countries.

- Japan—continues as the world leader in areas such as miniaturization, computer displays, memory chips, and manufacturing techniques but still lags in networking, application software, and systems integration.

- The United States—although the "hotbed" for digital technology and innovation in areas from communications and multimedia to biotech, microprocessing, and environmental technologies, there are growing concerns that weakness in public schools will cause the loss of the country's role as the world's center for new ideas.

RETHINKING GLOBAL ACCOUNTABILITY

Nowadays, accounting to the public for actions and results, both individual and corporate, has become the norm. The Information Age made all metrics of performance instant and global. In education, test scores of student achievement become relevant only when compared internationally; in business, measuring domestic market share has given way to measures of global share. Walter Wriston calls this the "information standard," and it's a new dimension to be factored into rethinking every strategy, plan, and action.

In health care, for example, patients have increasing on-line access to medical outcomes, patient satisfaction information, and financial data for both providers (HMOs, hospitals, clinics, and the like) and physicians. Medical patients in Massachusetts are able, in a matter of seconds, to find a surgeon's "success rate" from a centralized database using a toll-free 800 number. The Internet even has a site that rates the burgeoning number of health care sites. The availability of such information is destined to increase exponentially in the United States and eventually the world. In a world turned upside down, everyone, both organizations and individuals, will be "graded" against global benchmarks, and the results will be universally available.

Where such benchmarks don't exist today, new ones will be created and widely communicated. In financial services, for example, an innovative new company, Investment Scorecard, is creating a benchmark to measure, or "grade," investment performance. Founded in 1994, the company offered something no one else had, objective benchmarking for investors. Investment Scorecard provides its clients with a third-party "performance report card" that graphically and numerically communicates the financial results of their investment portfolios in a fast, easy, and comprehensive way.

On an individual level, we've long thought of competing in local, regional, or national job markets. Today, the employment market is international, and the job seeker must meet global standards, not narrow local standards. For many years corporate leaders recognized that manufacturing and marketing in a borderless world needed to be completely rethought. Corporations originally crossed national boundaries to find a broader customer base, source raw materials and parts, provide quality manufacturing at the lowest cost, and find cheaper money to finance growth. Now they also search globally to find, attract, and retain an educated, creative, and productive work force, which is, despite the world's six billion people, the scarcest of corporate commodities. Along with their global production and marketing presence, companies such as Nestle's, BASF, and Asea Brown Boveri boast multinational boards, officers, and employees of all ranks. The global employment search is at its most intense among U.S.-based high-tech firms, short nearly 200,000 software programmers. Software companies are going farther afield to find talent. Indeed, many are setting up offshore computer-programming facilities to take advantage of lower labor costs abroad, as well as recruiting programmers overseas to work in the United States. India has long been a recruiting target, but lately it is reportedly "overrun" with recruiters.

RETHINKING MONEY

Even money itself needs to be rethought. As Dee Hock, former CEO of Visa, has said, "Money has evolved from shells to green paper to the artful arrangement of binary digits." Digitized money and electronic financial services are revolutionizing the concept of money for consumers, both individual and corporate. Today, customers often consider the *kind* of money involved in a transaction as important as the transaction itself. Today, there are at least a half dozen kinds of money, among them what bankers are calling *daylight money, digital money, bank-linked electronic money,* and *corporate barter flows.*

As ATMs and smart cards pop up everywhere and banks

scramble to connect electronically with businesses and consumers worldwide, digital or electronic money challenges the traditional customer-bank relationship. Convenience and flexibility are the key.

Mobile banking, 24-hour global service, and electronic access to international money transfer are but a few of the new demands customers are making worldwide, and banks are finding innovative ways to address those needs. Visa advertises its Global Card Service as usable "any time, anywhere, any language." Recently, Spain's Banco Santandman, Goldman Sachs, the Royal Bank of Scotland, and EDS (Electronic Data Systems) teamed up to form Inter-Bank On-Line Systems (IBOS), which can reduce the time needed to transfer funds anywhere in the world to a mere seven seconds.

Citibank has become the world's first global consumer bank with operations in 100 countries, 60 of which are emerging markets. It has a long-established presence in the traditionally less attractive banking areas, such as the Caribbean, Latin America, and the Middle East, and now receives some 48 percent of its $4.2 billion (1997) revenues from its global consumer bank. It offers consumers around the world not just local banking services but sophisticated international ones as well. In Hong Kong, Citibank offers customers accounts in ten different currencies and provides hotline access to exchange rates or money transfers. Huntington Bancshares of Ohio provides videoconferencing kiosks for 24-hour customer access to banking staff and information in a variety of areas, from loans to mutual funds.

Typically today, only minor transactions (under $10) are enacted in cash. Smart cards and debit cards will largely eliminate even these in-store transactions. On the Internet, a number of companies—DEC, Microsoft, and Netscape among them—are now offering the electronic equivalent of coins and bills. Together with CyberGold, DigiCash (E-cash), and CyberCash (Cybercoin), these companies provide electronic "script" in "digital wallets" stored on a hard drive.

Daily electronic funds transfers now equal one-third of the U.S. annual GDP. Digital money clearly exceeds paper money as the grease of the economy, with over 90 percent of the value of all financial transactions coming from electronic transfers. As digital cash joins other major forms of electronic payments, paper and metal money will virtually disappear.

E-MONEY FOR THE E-WALLET

A 1997 full-page ad by IBM announces the transformation of the economy by electronic commerce and asks, "Are you ready?" Are you?

Using *Intranets*—Internet-like services deployed *within* an organization—and *Extranets*—a restricted portion of an organization's internal computer network opened up for customer or supplier use—electronic commerce connects critical operation and financial systems with customers, suppliers, and vendors. Estimates are that electronic commerce will reach $200 to $300 billion by 2001. The grease of electronic commerce will be e-money, just as paper money shaped the old world of business.

Despite the often-voiced concerns about security in electronic commerce, e-money is here, and it is rapidly replacing traditional money in the *e-wallet,* or electronic wallet. E-money marks the latest evolution of money from barter to coins, from coins to paper money, and through the increasing abstraction of payment methods that included debit cards, smart cards, and digital cash. (See Exhibit 8.1.)

By 1995, over 90 percent of all financial transactions in the United States were made electronically, and daily electronic fund transfers equaled one-third of the annual GDP. And the United States is not even the leader in these developments. France and Canada are taking the most significant steps in replacing traditional money with e-money. A major new "player" in the electronic transfer of funds is the smart card. By 1995, more than 50 million smart cards were in use worldwide. France leads the way in this particular method of electronic funds transfer with over 30 million smart cards in use. The city of Guelph, Ontario, in Canada is experimenting with smart card technology as a complete replacement for cash.

Banks, the traditional source of money for consumers and commerce, are increasingly redirecting their attention away from bricks and mortar branches toward the global electronic network.

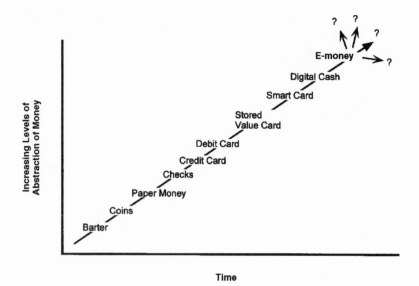

EXHIBIT 8.1   Money for the electronic wallet.

Canada's mbanx and Atlanta's Security First Network, for example, have no branches at all. They operate only electronically. Security First expects to be at a new account rate of 1000 per day by the year 2000. Ernst & Young estimates that the percentage of total U.S. bank transactions occurring in branches will fall from 56 percent in 1995 to 41 percent in 1998. Even those branches that still exist are migrating toward small corners of grocery stores and other high-traffic locations.

RETHINKING HOW FAST IS FAST

For perspective: Eight and a quarter minutes from the sun to the earth is the speed of light. Confirmed in 1848, for the past 150 years, this was believed to be the fastest speed possible. Scientists have discovered, however, that expanding rings around lightning charges actually spread outward at *three times the speed of light*.

In a recent issue, *Business Week* predicted a number of exciting changes in digital technology that by the year 2010 will require us to rethink everything about how fast is fast, how small is small, how cheap is cheap, and how smart is smart.

Among them:

• Chips with a quarter-billion transistors capable of putting supercomputer power into a credit-card sized device, hand-held videophones, human voice response computers, 3-D photo realism for virtual reality games and videoconferencing, and computers powered by light.

• Smart software management of computer networks too large and complex to tolerate human control. Software that will control everything from automobile suspensions to urban traffic systems to global information systems. The development of generic algorithms, which will make possible the ability to evolve and adapt quickly to change without the need for new programming.

• Chips capable of holding a billion bits; replacement of CD-ROM by small recordable disks capable of storing a library; the mainstreaming of experimental storage techniques such as holography.

• Telecom transmission speeds measured in trillions of bits per second and replacement of audio communications by video.

Rethinking how fast is fast won't wait until 2010 however. In a late 1997 newspaper ad, Nortel described how fast is fast and how much is a lot. The company claimed that their high-capacity fiber-optic bandwidth product line could deliver 160 gigabytes per second over a single fiber. That's more than 60 times the voice, multimedia, and Internet communications-carrying capacity of most current networks." At the individual chip level, researchers are now projecting low-cost memory chips that store 1000 times more information and communicate 100 times faster than current ones. IBM began shipping a new, faster chip in early 1998 that is 20 percent cheaper and 40 percent more powerful than its previous designs. It's not just the computer business that's rethinking how fast is fast. In late 1997, a 110,000 horsepower "car" not only broke the land speed record (at 763.035 miles per hour) but also went supersonic, breaking the sound barrier just 50 years after an airplane had done so.

EVERY CELL
A FACTORY

A 1997 *Business Week* cover article pointed out that the twentieth century witnessed the ascendancy of physics with the splitting of the atom, the exploration of relativity and quantum theory, and the harnessing of the power of silicon chips. The article predicts medical, environmental, and agricultural advances, and even the expanded potential of biotech to include the application of gene splicing and genome engineering to the creation of more powerful computing. Indeed, bio-materials represent the next logical step in the evolution of science and technology, and the production of such materials will "flip" us from our current economic era of information to a new and dramatically different one. The real "high tech" of today is not information management but biotechnology and new materials.

The roots of biotechnology go back to 1665, when British scientist Robert Hooke coined the word *cell*. Notwithstanding several centuries worth of progress in biology, the next relevant event, for this account, at least, took place in 1953, when British scientists James Watson and Francis Crick described the anatomy of DNA—the double helix. Scientists worldwide are now working off this basic discovery.

While the early importance of biotech will be in agriculture and medical applications, the long-range impact will be in the production of commercial goods. The commercialization of bio-materials amounts to companies manipulating the biological structure of matter, such as DNA and cell culture, for commercial human uses. Universities and corporations throughout the world are investing more effort and money in research and development of biotech products. Large chemical and pharmaceutical companies are rapidly acquiring or forming partnerships with small, innovative biotech startup companies. Biotech companies appear to be at about the same stage relative to bio-materials that IBM and other computer-technology developers were in the 1950s.

The potential for biotechnology and bio-materials to transform our notions of products, services, materials, and even life itself is phenomenal, and as scientists and others have pointed out, we have scarcely scratched the surface. A July 1996 article in *Professional Engineering* predicted that biotechnology would "soon become just as important to a wide range of industry as the steam engine or the microprocessor," with applications in the engineering, food, chemicals, metals, textiles, paper, and environmental industries.

BIO-MATERIALS: THE NEXT ECONOMIC ERA

Biotechnology will demonstrate again that the technology of each new economic era transforms everything that came before it. Chapter 2 described how the mechanical "muscle" power of Industrial Age technologies revolutionized agriculture, and the intellectual "brainpower" of Information Age technologies— robotics, CAD-CAM, CIM, etc.—is now revolutionizing manufacturing on factory floors throughout the world. We can expect no less of technologies of the future. In fact, Bio-Material Age technologies already hold the promise of revolutionizing not only agriculture (with new types of plants, etc.) but also Industrial Age manufacturing technologies, by creating new materials and *biological production processes*. Already, scientists are working on a "biological computer" to overcome the physical limitations of the materials in use today.

Chapter 2 also asserted that each economic era creates a view of the world or paradigm that is hard to reconcile with the

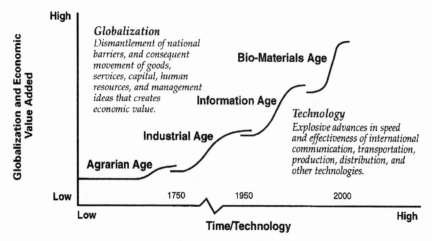

EXHIBIT 9.1 Bio-materials: the new engine of the economy. Two major forces create the global village: technology and globalization.

advent of a new era. This is particularly true during the initial transition from one economic era to the next. Early in the Information Age, for example, the manufacturing paradigm of mass customization seemed virtually impossible to those unable to see beyond the Industrial Age paradigm of mass production. And while many have clung to the Industrial Age idea of economies of scale, its importance has been eclipsed by the importance of economies of scope.

Each era, likewise, seems to have achieved a fundamental transformation. The Agricultural Age conquered hunger, for example. The Industrial Age conquered space, and the Information Age conquered time. The Bio-Materials Age now promises to conquer matter. In 1994, scientists at the Fermi National Accelerator Laboratory in Chicago believed they had briefly caught sight, through their lab detector, of what scientists have tagged the "top quark," the basic building block of matter. Confirmation of this historic sighting and subsequent experimentation with the basic building blocks of matter will alter our global views of wealth, natural resources, and value. For example, simply targeting change within a single protein can produce dramatic results in terms of the quality, quantity, and costs of new and existing products.

Although current biotech efforts are most often associated with agricultural and medical products, the ultimate impact will be to recreate the very idea of the factory.

AGRICULTURE: IN PURSUIT OF THE PERFECT PLANT

Advances in biotech are quickly beginning to provide answers to many of the world's agricultural dilemmas. While many people scorn the manipulation of cells in both plants and animals as "playing God," the potential benefits are enormous—"the biggest thing since mechanized power," one agricultural economist exclaimed.

New products have proliferated rapidly. By the end of 1994, Calgene's gene-altered "Flavr Savr" tomato was available in more than 700 stores. In this tomato, scientists blocked the genes that initiate rot, allowing the tomato to ripen fully before harvesting and creating a more attractive, juicier, better-tasting vegetable that withstands the rigors of shipping. In other words, the tomato was biologically altered to enhance the distribution process instead of being altered negatively because of it. Genetically manipulated potatoes and other vegetables are already in the works, including low-fat chips from genetically altered soybeans.

In recent years, genetic research has led to the development of crop varieties that have obtained U.S. government approval. Monsanto is a world leader in the development of such products, with its Yield Gard corn, New Leaf potatoes, and Roundup Ready soybeans. The company's biotech green plant products are projected to reach more than $6 billion in revenues by 2005. In its enthusiasm for agri-biotech, Monsanto has created joint ventures with other companies and jumped in to save Calgene's struggling Flavr Savr tomato when production problems threatened its future. Not all biotech efforts involve corporate giants or high-profile crops, though. For example, in Saskatoon, Saskatchewan, Prairie Systems, Inc., is focusing its efforts on the development and production of a biotech berry.

Many of the new green plants developed in biotech labs are proving to be drought resistant. Of even greater significance perhaps is the development of a whole new generation of pest controls based on biotech and genetic engineering. This rapidly advancing agricultural revolution promises to substantially transform farming and provide greater value for global consumers, and it also addresses the realities of massive world population growth.

MEDICINE: CREATING THE BIONIC BODY

The major focus in medicine is the race among leading pharmaceutical/genomics companies to discover the genetic functions affecting cancer, HIV, Alzheimer's, and other diseases and to use this knowledge to create potential cures for these dreaded diseases. In addition to pure research and medical applications, cell therapy, gene-mapping, and genetic engineering hold promise for scores of industries as well.

The most dramatic and highly publicized research is the Human Genome Project, the goal of which is to map and sequence over 100,000 human genes. By the mid-1990s, only about 2 percent (or 2000 genes) had been successfully located and mapped by scientists, but a complete "map" is expected within a couple of years into the new century. While mapping gene location on the chromosome is critical for understanding genetic influences on human health, including mental health, the critical task lies in the sequential placement of those genes (over three billion base pairs per set of twenty-three chromosomes).

Scientist Leroy Hood points to three categories into which biological information falls: digital (one-dimensional) DNA information, the three-dimensional formation of proteins, and the four-dimensional information of complex systems and networks. Although DNA research absorbs the bulk of university scientific efforts, medical biotech is increasingly focusing on the second and third categories. For example, at the University of New Mexico researchers, led by Mo Shahinpoor, created artificial muscles out of latex sheaths encapsulated in fibers of polyacrylonitrile. Altering the PH solution which is pumped through the fibers forces contraction of the substitute muscle.

Meanwhile, researchers in Boston are engineering living human tissue and creating surrogates for human body parts—everything from skin to heart valves and arteries—"from scratch." In another area, the Food and Drug Administration is closing in on approval of tissue engineering. Researchers already boast that these new "cells are so smart that all the complexity of tissues doesn't have to be created from scratch. We just have to give them the right clues." In many cases, parts from genetically engineered pigs are being used as replacements for human tissues and organs. Scientific experimentation in these areas has improved to the point that by 2010, an estimated 450,000 pig organs will serve human medical needs.

While such issues are grabbing headlines and stirring ethics controversies, the general public is most familiar with biotech's potential in the area of pharmaceutical product development for fighting disease. Following recent revelations of new strains of bacteria, the revival of many diseases such as tuberculosis and malaria, and the spread of bacterial resistance to many antibiotics, universities and pharmaceutical research teams are now approaching the development of new medicines with increased urgency. Much of this research is again honing in on genes and proteins to learn secrets that will assist in fighting disease.

ENVIRONMENT: TURNING POLLUTION INTO GOLD

Biotechnology research is addressing other health concerns by discovering ways to use bacteria to solve environmental problems. Using a method reminiscent of the old Pac Man games, biotechnologists uncovered a way of using bacteria to gobble up pollutants. Technically sophisticated, the process—*membrane biotreatment*—collects and clears toxins produced by industrial exhaust. Not surprisingly, innovators in these efforts include major polluters, such as the furniture industry, which is required by federal law to find ways to cut down on fumes. A variety of industries in other countries are utilizing biofilters to stem the flow of pollutants. The Mercedes-Benz plant between Stuttgart and Esslingen, Germany, installed a biofilter with the capacity to purify 320,000 cubic meters of fumes per hour, thanks to a bacterial composition housed in vats of wood shavings.

Advances in biotechnology have also encouraged synergies among companies in which the waste from one can be used as raw material in the manufacturing processes of another. In Kalundborg, Denmark, for example, a number of businesses— a power plant, an oil refinery, a maker of cement, a fish farm, and local residents—share waste products to provide energy sources for each other. By understanding the potential value of waste products for other companies, an organization can share economic benefits while producing a positive impact on local ecology.

Bio-products from charcoal and wood have also been channeled into energy for much of the developing world. While these fuel systems have not been widely used in the United States, there is a growing interest in bio-fuels in the rest of the industrial world.

While the wonders of biotechnology are already evident through the efforts of small innovative companies and university research labs to improve the environment, pharmaceuticals, health care, and agriculture, its most far-reaching impact will happen on the factory floor with the creation of commercial and consumer bio-materials.

BIO-MATERIALS: EVERY CELL A FACTORY

The creation of new food, medicine, and ecological products will continue to grab the early attention in biotech, and rightly so. But it is the conversion of this science to commercial applications that will create the greatest economic advances. The signs are already evident.

High-tech computerization, for example, is one major focus area of bio-materials scientists. At MIT, scientists are wedding computer technology with bio-materials technology through the development of a photonic bandgap microactivity resonator. The new process speeds and dramatically increases the flow of information along optical fibers by separating data streams and channeling them so that they can be processed simultaneously.

The excitement generated by the potential applications of biotech to computing is matched by recent discoveries in the transfer of photons in demonstrations of quantum teleportation, the shifting of physical characteristics from originals to replicas. Reminiscent of the "beam-me-up-Scottie" teleporting of Star Trek crew members, Anton Zeilinger and his colleagues at the University of Innsbruck decomposed and then transported bits of light (photons) from one place to another.

In a 1997 article for *The Sciences,* Marvin L. Cohen points out that these and similar efforts reinforce science's changing agenda toward the "perfecting of matter" through the exploration of its physical properties. Cohen contends that building conceptual models of solids will lead scientists to truly understand the physical properties of materials. Such understanding, he suggests, will permit scientists to move toward creating exotic materials that will break new ground in hardness, density, and conductivity.

Biotech scientists from The University of Michigan and James Madison University in Virginia, for example, are conducting research on a green plant that produces polyethylene resins, the feedstock for making plastic, currently only available as a product of "cracking" oil. These scientists have discovered a cheaper process. Soil microorganisms contain a plastic-producing gene which, when inserted into a plant cell, produces biodegradable plastic. This new biotech polyethylene resin has many of the properties of the current product with the advantage, as a natural substance, of being biodegradable. Imagine the implications of the power of American agriculture being applied to "growing" plastics.

At Cornell University, scientists are experimenting with a "spider factory" and are attempting to harvest spider webs. The web material has a higher tensile strength than steel, and the Cornell researchers hope to learn how to produce it commercially for applications such as sailcloth. In the meantime, Cornell's "spider factory" manager notes, "Spiders are great, they work for free, and they don't take vacations."

Creating new materials with spiders is not just the province of a university lab focused on the future. DuPont Company scientists are using biosilk as the model for a new generation of materials. In recent ads, the company touts the "strength and stretch" of spider silk, calling it the strongest material known, a single strand able, they say, to "stop a 747 in flight." In one recent ad, apparently aimed at developing awareness of the value of biosilk, the company proclaimed that spiker silk "has the potential to transform our lives in countless ways we can scarcely imagine...Based upon the success of our initial demonstrations, we believe that harnessing biosynthesis will play a major role in the new materials revolution."

Similar strength and flexibility might likewise be found in marine mussels. Scientists are now investigating the molecular structure of the mussel and its potential for development as "artificial scaffolding" for the repair of human tendons, as well as other sea creatures for the incredible strength of their shells and the hold of their "glues."

In an attempt to keep pace with the growing demand for wood and paper products, scientists for companies like Union Camp Corporation and Wesvaco are working to create the "super-tree," a lab-engineered specimen that can grow 100 feet in ten years, withstand disease, and produce more wood. Through selective breeding, these super-trees will be engineered to resemble sticks, without excess branches and leaves. Genetics is the key to unlocking the secret of growth rate in trees, and timber scientists are rushing to discover the right formula in this potentially lucrative area. Such short-cycle tree production could lead to lower costs for all wood products.

The potential of such advances is augmented by the current development of some amazing products that are destined to impact our lives. Minimagnets (similar to magnetic "tweezers") will allow a single molecule to be directed through the body to a specific cell. A shirt-button-size battery will be capable of generating ten to twenty times more power than conventional computer batteries. These miniature (4 millimeter) turbine batteries look like a jet engine and could be mass produced like computer chips.

ETHICAL DILEMMAS: TO CLONE OR NOT TO CLONE?

Advances in biotechnology may answer many commercial challenges, but they also carry an assortment of risks. Although monies and investment are now flowing briskly into bio-materials, the industry is under heavy attack from critics who fear the outcome of tampering with nature's laws. Some legislation or industry self-regulation may result as biotech scientists move further into agricultural biotech and closer to altering life forms. While such concerns should not be dismissed lightly, the many positive outcomes of bioengineering also should not be discounted.

Major questions regarding allowing genetically engineered products into the environment and the marketplace are already on the public agenda. All other controversy pales, however, compared to the recent drama surrounding the successful cloning of a sheep named "Dolly," by Scottish embryologist Ian Wilmut. Dolly evoked world reaction ranging from awe to outrage and a rush to create legislation to control this new power over nature. The event was a wake-up call on our ability to manipulate life on earth. Within months of the successful experiment, activists voiced their concerns about all manifestations of biotech agricultural development, and the U.S. Congress began debating cloning, animal and human.

Television news and other press reports soon expanded coverage of all aspects of biotechnology. There are no easy answers, nor will answers soon be forthcoming. Whether or not specific prohibitions should or will be developed is beyond the scope of this book. It is important to remember, however, that as research proceeds globally, no one country can effectively control the direction or pace of biotech development. Activities banned by one country will simply move to another. The hope is that rational approaches to bio-materials development will be articulated and agreed upon globally.

While we are early in this cycle, seeing the ultimate potential for products of the Bio-Materials Age remains as illusive as foretelling the future of the computer was during the 1950s. One thing is clear, though. Bio-material products and processes will alter virtually everything that has come before them. The slope of the "S" curve for the Bio-Materials Age will be steep and its impact will be huge. Nor will it be a phenomenon of a few countries; it will happen globally. While the economic impact of bio-materials is yet to be known, one thing is crystal clear: *We are now firmly in the Age of Bio-Materials.*

As was pointed out in Part 1, each new economic era also creates dramatically higher levels of economic value added and takes us to new levels of global integration. We can expect that the new technologies of the coming decades will create unprecedented levels of wealth and help usher in an extended period of economic prosperity with concomitant global integration and stability.

2050 A.D.

What happens after the Bio-Materials Age? One possibility is that there will be a relatively tranquil, flatter S-curve period and a new engine of economic growth, "Edutainment Age." Edutainment is a term already in use. Near the end of the Information Age, it was coined to capture the coming together of the educational and entertainment industries, and more specifically, a new type of "content" that is at once educational and entertaining.

This period may well appear "tranquil" because its outward manifestations would seem calm compared to a century or more of conquering space, time, and matter. The reason for the relatively flat slope and extended duration of The Edutainment Age is that human "internal" changes occur at a much slower rate than the "external" environmental changes of past economic eras. (See Exhibit E.1.)

This new economic era will have more to do with what's in our heads than with competition to satisfy our creature comforts. Most everyone is familiar with Maslow's "Hierarchy of Needs" and its triangle diagram with "self-actualization" perched atop the pyramid. In the twenty-first century, we will come to see this pyramid, like the rest of the world, turned upside down, as portrayed in Exhibit E.2. The quest for self-actualization—in all its forms—will become the world's biggest industry. In fact, if the tourism industry were included, the edutainment business would already be the world's largest. Combined, education and entertainment businesses today account for some $770 billion in the United States alone. At 14 percent of GDP, this rivals spending on health care.

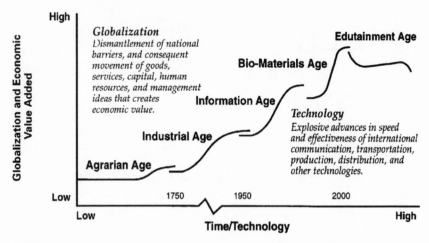

EXHIBIT E.1   Edutainment: economic engine in mid-twenty-first century.

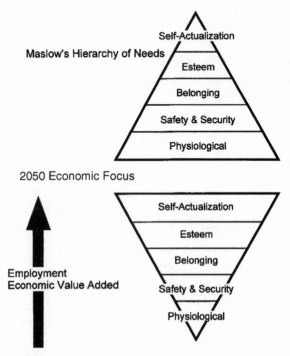

EXHIBIT E.2   Edutainment: employment and economic value added in 2050.

The Edutainment Age will be an era in which intellectual pursuits will, in part, mask commercial ones; technologies will make education so entertaining that it will be hard to distinguish work from play; the development of intellectual capital will be so dominant a commercial goal that employees will essentially spend full-time learning new skills. In other words entertaining education will be the key economic driver of the economy. It will not be utopia, however, because edutainment will be pursued vigorously and competitively.

Edutainment will be like a global computer game, engaging virtually everyone around the globe in high involvement at high stakes. Much of edutainment will be "second-hand reality" conducted via the global communications infrastructure, and will create an era of "electronic tribalism." With the advent of the global village in the late 1960s, people became increasingly group and team-oriented in their outlook and work patterns. This new group orientation was visible as many individual efforts at work gave way to empowered work teams. Geo-politically, it was expressed in the growth of new ethnically defined countries. During the Edutainment Age, this trend will continue and extend to other parts of life, culminating in what might be called "electronic ethnicity."

"ELECTRONIC ETHNICITY" JOINS TRADITIONAL ETHNICITY

With the low cost and ease of global communications brought about by the Internet in the mid-1990s, people quickly became part of globally dispersed, electronic communities, whose members were united not by geography, culture, race, language, or religion but by common interests shared in cyberspace. These "virtual villages" or "virtual communities" sprang up everywhere and were unbounded by all the traditional ties.

In this new electromechanical *space,* there is no centralized authority and no business rules. Therefore, the electronic village creates new challenges and opportunities for businesses. Many of them are dominated by discussions of particular products and services. By the late 1990s, marketers were seeing the need to aggressively participate in these electronic chat groups. A number of companies, for instance, assigned marketing professionals full-time as participants in the global on-line chat networks created by the users of their equipment and services. Their jobs included correcting inaccurate information and exerting positive influence on user discussions about their products. The CEO of one company reported that in the first couple of months, several modifications to current products and at least two new product innovations came about as a result of monitoring the "electronic chat" about its products and those of its competitors. In the Information Age, businesses found it profitable to focus on ethnic groups rather than nationalities. In the Edutainment Age, businesses will find it more profitable to focus on electronically defined groups.

These new electronic groups, like their traditional ethnic counterparts, argue for their own space, only this time the space is not political or geographic. As with geographic space, however, the electromechanical spectrum is limited. Therefore, new "world" conflicts could arise between these groups over their respective share of the electromechanical spectrum.

TECHNOLOGY REDEFINES ETHNIC SPACE

As communications technologies increasingly impact all aspects of our lives in the Edutainment Age, we will witness a redefinition of individual identity beyond the biological and traditional social relationships of family, neighborhood, city, or nation to the development of new affinity groups based on interests shared via the network. Just as transportation technologies, particularly the automobile and the jet engine, transformed ideas of physical and geographic space, the Internet and related technologies will transform our concept of spatial consciousness. Cyberspace will replace physical space in creating our feelings of "belonging." As individuals spend increasing amounts of their time on the Net, they will become more isolated from their traditional family or ethnic roots. Electronically enabled affinity groups on the Net will allow people to develop strong new "ethnic" attachments in the electromechanical spectrum. They will be "virtual beings," who operate independent of time and geography. This "virtual ethnic" may be only a nodding acquaintance to a neighbor across the street but will think nothing of chatting for hours on the Net with "electronic comrades," say fellow biking enthusiasts whom he or she has never met and probably never will.

In addition to creating new challenges for business, these groups have begun rewriting the rules of politics as well. In the U.S. Presidential primary elections in 1996, for example, candidates set up extensive web sites to provide voters with real-time, in-depth information about their candidacies. Thus, the battle of politics on the Net became official, and it has continued to grow in the years since, with all kinds of political party and independent chat groups debating all manner of political issues. By the year 2000, American politicians will find that cyberspace will have as profound an impact on the Presidential election as TV did in 1960.

Because of their complex global composition, many of these new ethnic groups defy categorization by traditional standards. United by an idea, members may be unaware of the traditional ethnic makeup of others in the group. Similar to traditional ethnic designations, however, this new form of reference group will largely determine how and with whom members relate, what they believe in, and in some extreme cases, what they are prepared to defend and how vigorously.

It is likely, though, that the whole nature of conflict as we have known it—physical, geographically based, and critically dependent on natural resources—will be transformed into conflicts over access to presence in electronic space—based on technological resources and network. Thus the Net may hasten the demise of wars between atoms and usher in a new era of wars between bits.

RETHINKING THINKING FOR THE EDUTAINMENT AGE

Contemplating the potential for electronic warfare in the middle of the next century may be a stretch. However, one aspect of this era that will surely be rethought is that of thinking itself, because the most important battles of this new era will occur inside people's heads.

By the early 1990s, rapid technological advances and expanding global markets marked a shift in the pattern of thought—away from the left-brain dominance of visual space described earlier in this book toward an equality between left brain (abstract, verbal, analytical, logical, linear, and sequential) and right brain (associative, nonverbal, holistic, creative, flexible, and chaotic).

Prior to the invention of the phonetic alphabet, ideas were communicated orally or through pictures, simple ideographs and icons, the latter often representing complex ideas in a single simple image. Today, neurological scientists know that such communication—oral, graphic, and iconic—primarily engages the right hemisphere of the brain. Print, on the other hand, with its abstract linearity, engages the left side or hemisphere of the brain. Thus, the widespread adoption of reading in the western world emphasized the left brain and consequentially led to the development and eventual dominance of casual logic. Sequence, precision, centralized command and control, discipline, and order became highly valued. Linear thinking reached its ultimate expression in the mass production of the Industrial Age, the conveyor belt moving identical products along a line for the sequential addition of parts. Left-brain values also dominated the "scientific" education process, while the right brain was seen as the preserve of "artistic" expression. However, by 1997 neuroscientists concluded that they had reached the point where they could understand the cellular basis of cognition. And although still debatable, there seems to be some agreement that domain-specific regions of the brain do exist and that highly complex problems, of the type that will be encountered in edutainment, induce activity in the left as well as the right side of the brain.

The volume of print media, in combination with the growing pervasiveness of electronic media will surround the individual in a torrent of information. In the Information Age we began to measure information in gigabits; in the Edutainment Age it will be in terabits (10^{12}) and petabits (10^{15}). At such enormous volumes, information content gets incredibly complex.

INFORMATION COMPLEXITY

As we exit the twentieth century, the global telecommunications network has perhaps the world's most complex system. Yet for users worldwide, it is among the easiest to use. It epitomizes a cardinal rule of high-tech business today: user-simple, chooser-complex. In this case the "choosers" are companies that own and operate this increasingly complex network. But even for some the world's most highly sophisticated telecommunications engineers, the complexity is approaching a stage that demands a new way of thinking. This new way of thinking is manifested in a whole new series of network management tools from industry suppliers that are designed to convert huge volumes of linear information—on network use or customer behavior for example. Called *data visualization*, these tools have the ability to quickly render large amounts of information in easy-to-understand patterns of information.

Pattern recognition, particularly visual, will become a premium thinking style. The first signs of the importance of pattern recognition appeared with the complexity of computer programs. As discussed in Chapter 7, Apple computer software programmers found, for example, that large amounts of information could be represented by icons that are easily recognized and used by anyone. Known as *graphical user interface* (GUI), it gave them an early market edge and has since been employed by Microsoft Windows. Even software programmers themselves, faced with an ever-growing mass of software code, have adopted an "object-oriented" language in which a single visual object represents a vast body of linear code. Such holistic, nonverbal, iconic communication tools engage right-brain skills like intuition, spontaneity, symbolism, and visual recognition.

As the volume of information grows exponentially, attempts to use new ways of thinking, primarily visual and iconic, will continue to grow as well. It is perhaps no surprise that 3D imaging is the hottest and fastest growing area of software development, or that holography is finding its way into more and more commercial applications. A hologram is at once a simple image and one that carries large amounts of information—multiple visual images, all with a different perspective and depth. In fact, you could say that a hologram is worth a thousand pictures. Holography may well represent the best way to think about the geometrically accumulating amounts of information that await us in the Edutainment Age.

FROM "COG IN THE WHEEL" TO "NODE IN THE NETWORK"

Near the end of the Industrial Age, Charley Chaplin used one of the most clever inventions, the movie camera, to produce the film *Modern Times,* which portrayed the worst abuses of the industrial era. In one classic scene, Chaplin's character, a factory worker, gets trapped in the wheel of the production machinery, which is driven ever faster by a maniacal manager. In many ways the scene captured the sense of powerlessness, the cog-in-the-wheel feeling experienced by many during this period, when machines seem to dominate man.

Many feel that the inventions of the Information Age, the computer in particular, are even more dangerous in this regard. However, those critics fail to see a primary aspect of information technology: It's an extension of human intelligence. They also miss the dramatic shift, visible now in virtually every walk of life, from passive recipient to active participant. In other words, this technology has transformed us from audience to actor in events that rule our lives. In the past, we were often little more than passive receivers of mass messages or the powerless audience for products and ideas. However, personal and interactive technologies, innovations in bio-materials, and eventually edutainment technologies, empower us as full participants. As demonstrated in Chapters 6 and 7, customers have become empowered, engaged, and actively integrated into the business organization's decision-making process. Likewise, technologies have transformed corporate thinking from the notion of worker as "machine" to worker as "intelligent participant," with shared leadership and responsibility in reaching common goals.

With the explosion of low-cost, widespread interactive technologies such as the Internet, the notions of "community" or "network" will be extended further and further, beyond countries and organizations alike, breaking down old barriers and paving the way for individual power, inclusiveness, and collaboration. Once the genie of inclusion and power is out of the bottle, there is no getting it back in. The shape of the new world of business is being fundamentally transformed. Every individual is becoming an essential "node in the network."

It is impossible to summarize with any degree of succinctness a book that has charted such a wide course through history and across the globe. The book has attempted to help the reader look forward to the shape of things to come, and to provide some context by trying to make sense of the last fifty years, and more particularly, the last ten. Perhaps it will suffice to say that the vast changes of the past were simply practice for what lies ahead.

ABOUT THE AUTHOR

Richard W. Oliver is a professor at the Owen Graduate School of Management at Vanderbilt University in Nashville, Tennessee. He was previously Vice President of Marketing at Nortel and a marketing executive at DuPont. Dr. Oliver serves on the Boards of Directors of six U.S. companies and consults to organizations around the world. He is the coauthor, with William Jenkins, of the 1998 best-seller *The Eagle and the Monk: 7 Principles of Successful Change.*

INDEX